Advertising Strategy

Advertising Strategy

A 360 Degree Brand Approach

Larry D. Kelley
Kim Bartel Sheehan

Melvin & Leigh, Publishers
IRVINE, CALIFORNIA

Advertising Strategy: A 360 Degree Brand Approach

Published by Melvin & Leigh, Publishers
6 Curie Court
Irvine, CA 92617

orders.melvinleigh@cox.net
www.melvinleigh.com

Cover design by Jesse Sanchez
Production by Stacey Victor

ISBN: 978-0-99730845-7

Printed in the United States of America on mixed recycle paper

Visit our home page at www.melvinleigh.com

Table of Contents

Preface and Acknowledgments

A strategically-developed, integrated, brand communications campaign is the cornerstone of a brand's success. Yet, until now, there has not been a book that takes a holistic view of integrated marketing communications. Most advertising strategy and advertising books focus on creative strategy and execution. Other books that impact advertising strategy are very specialized, such as media strategy, promotional strategy, or social media strategy. Marketing strategy books discuss all the aspects of marketing with advertising typically treated as just the promotional part of a brand.

Advertising Strategy: A 360 Degree Brand Approach provides a comprehensive approach to all the factors related to crafting an integrated brand communication plan. This book is devoted to strategy. As you will see, the text is heavily invested in "how" as opposed to "what." It is much more prescriptive than descriptive. At every stage of the integrated brand communication process, the book focuses on how the brand gains the maximum benefit based on the strategic decisions made.

The book works from the inside out connecting all strategic brand decisions. Marketing decisions form the first layer. Consumer insights form the next layer. The central idea is the next layer followed by messaging and media strategies. Each strategy builds upon the other. The best integrated brand communication plans are intertwined rather than discrete tasks.

The text is designed to provide a 360 degree brand communication viewpoint. This includes brand promotion as well as brand protection. In today's brand media world of instant consumer feedback, it is crucial to understand not only how communication can be used to promote the brand but how communication can be used to defend the brand's reputation.

Differing situations demand different strategies. The book details how to view strategic decisions in the midst of various situations from competitive intrusion to the introduction of a new brand. Brands are susceptible to different cultures and geographic nuances. The book discusses how to develop global strategies that can be adjusted to local market conditions.

Within the ever-changing field of integrated brand communication, there are more reasons than ever to have a "go-to" source that provides a complete view of brand communication decisions. Brand managers, who have little formal training in communication planning, students of advertising, integrated communication, and marketing programs, and other practioners such as agency account managers, account planners, and media salespeople can all benefit from this book's content and application focus.

Acknowledgments

The authors wish to thank Harry Briggs, our publisher and co-founder of Melvin & Leigh Publishers for giving us the opportunity to publish this book. We would also like to thank the Melvin & Leigh team, including our production editor, Stacey Victor, for their tireless work on this project. We also thank our spouses and families for all their support, without which the project would not have been possible.

Chapter 1

Advertising Strategy: A 360 Degree Brand Viewpoint

Learning Objectives

This chapter is intended to help you:

- Learn the definition of strategy
- Learn the origin of strategy
- Understand the definition of strategy for brand communication
- Understand the 360 degree brand viewpoint

What Is Strategy?

In a classic Dilbert cartoon created by Adam Scott, Dilbert's pointed-haired boss asks Dilbert when his plan will be done. Dilbert replies, "I can't do it until you give me the strategy." And without missing a beat, his boss says, "My strategy is to make you do a plan."

As this cartoon illustrates, strategy is a concept that can be overused and many times not well understood. This is particularly true in the field of integrated brand communication. Much of this confusion stems from the fact that brand communication is typically done by a variety of people and/or companies. For instance, you may have a media planning agency, a creative agency, a digital agency, an internal social media team, a web team, a public relations agency, and a promotions agency. Compounding the confusion is that the brand positioning and marketing may be influenced by many internal stakeholders as well as groups of outside brand, marketing, and business consultants. They all are developing plans. Are these plans strategic? Do they work in concert or do they view strategy through their own areas of expertise? How do we determine if these plans are strategic? What is the strategy?

Let's start with a review of how Webster defines "strategy." The first tip that strategy can be misunderstood is that Webster has three definitions for this word. There is no single definition. It depends upon your perspective.

Webster first defines strategy as "a careful plan or method to achieve a goal over a long period of time." This is one way to view strategy. It is a plan to achieve an objective. Objectives are defined as long-term goals. So strategy is **how** you are going to get it done. However, under this definition, any plan that is designed to achieve the objective can be viewed as strategic. There is no distinction from one plan to another.

The second definition is, "the art and science of employing a cohesive set of complex forces to support adopted policies." This definition comes from the political world. Here strategy is the coordination of various factors, such as economic, social, political, and military, from a single country, group of countries, single organization, or group of organizations to support a policy. For example, if the United States government's policy is to isolate North Korea, then the strategy or way to accomplish this is to apply various economic, political, and social sanctions with the threat of military force coordinated through the United Nations. While this is a very distinct definition for political science, it is a difficult fit outside that realm.

The third Webster definition is, "the art and science of military command designed to meet the enemy in combat under advantageous conditions." This definition is very specific to the military. It is the definition of military strategy. Just like the definition for political science, this definition is focused on a specific type of strategy.

While none of these definitions by themselves are a perfect fit for our topic, there is much to learn from each of these three definitions that impact brand communication. First, you need a plan. The operative word is "a" plan. Not a series of plans. You have an objective. A strategy is the way to meet this objective. The first definition is all about focus. Second, you have the aspect of the political definition. This is where we learn that the plan must be cohesive and may contain a complex set of forces. In the case of brand communication, this can be a complex set of brand communication methods and/or tactics. Finally, third is from the military definition of strategy, "advantageous." In military combat, the strategy is designed to provide a combat advantage in the field of battle. The plan has a point of view. It is not merely a plan to get from point A to point B. This plan seeks to gain an advantage over the "enemy."

As we review these three definitions of strategy, they work together to begin to paint a picture of what integrated brand communication strategy is all about. It is a singular plan that requires cohesive coordination of a variety of elements that gives the brand an advantage in the marketplace.

With this in mind, let's take a brief look at the history of strategy and how it can impact brand communication.

Origins of Strategy

The origin of strategy begins with evolutionary biology. From the dawn of time, there has been a struggle to gain the resources needed for survival. If you aren't the biggest or the strongest, you need to find another way to survive. A way to accomplish this was to outsmart or outthink those who were physically more dominant. So, a fundamental element of strategy is "outsmarting the other guy." Strategy has its origins in seeking victory by using your head versus using your brawn.

If you think about brands and communication, each has its own series of struggles. For a brand, it is a struggle to get and keep the brand in the marketplace. And for communication, it is a struggle to gain and keep the attention of the audience. While neither a brand nor brand communication is a life or death struggle, the need to outthink and outsmart the competition is clearly the same as our ancestors many years ago.

Beyond the evolutionary idea of strategy, strategic thought largely comes from military strategy and battlefield conflicts. While we don't say that brand communication is anything remotely as serious as military warfare, there is a lot to learn from military strategy.

Sun Tzu's *The Art of War* from 500 BCE is the basis for a great deal of military and business strategy. There are many corporate leaders who have a copy of *The Art of War* on their bookshelves. Sun Tzu's approach to military strategy is greatly influenced by Taoist philosophy. As a result, the approach combines the best of battlefield strategy and tactics with a gentle art of statesmanship. The result is some timeless lessons that can be applied to a variety of business situations including integrated brand communication.

The following are some of the key ideas from *The Art of War* that have implications for brand communication strategy:

- It is better "to subdue the enemy without fighting than to win one hundred victories in one hundred battles."
- "Whoever is first in the field will be fresh and whoever is second will arrive exhausted."
- The key to deception is "simply a matter of doing the opposite of what is expected."

If a brand is so clearly positioned and its communication is equally clear on point, then other brands may elect to avoid that position or communication strategy. That is the essence of winning the fight without truly fighting. The lesson from Sun Tzu is that if you are perceived to be so dominant, you are unlikely to face a challenge. An example could be a brand such as Google, which dominates Internet search engines. Or, it could Absolut® Vodka, a brand that clearly occupies a unique niche and communication strategy in the vodka category. While there are brands that compete with these two brands, the competition may be reluctant to directly attack them.

Being first to market is truly an advantage in terms of brand communication. Just as Sun Tzu points out, the first mover is fresh and the second is exhausted. If we put that into brand communication terms, the first mover is still fresh while the second mover has to spend a lot more energy and money catching up to that first mover. It is always best to be first.

Conventional wisdom said that when Iraq invaded Kuwait in 1990, the best way for the United States to return Kuwait to freedom would be to directly attack the Iraqi army. It just made sense. The United States had more weapons, soldiers, and sophistication. However, General Norman Schwarzkopf had another idea that would potentially greatly reduce allied casualties. He feigned a direct attack on the key port of Kuwait while driving his army hundreds of miles through the desert to attack the Iraqi army from the rear—a surprise move. Operation Desert Storm was a huge success. It reversed the Iraqi occupation and had minimal casualties. It is a classic case of doing something unexpected.

The same can be said for Dove, which *Advertising Age* named the best campaign of the decade in 2015. Conventional wisdom says that you market beauty products by associating them with fashion models. Dove did the unexpected and associated the brand with real women. Their "Campaign for Real Beauty" flew in the face of the industry and propelled Dove to double-digit sales increases.

Carl von Clausewitz's book, *On War*, written in 1832 is another widely-referenced military strategy book that has made its way into the business world. Here are three of the key principles of war cited in his work:

- It is crucial to concentrate superior force or power at the decisive place and time.
- You should look for the element of surprise and strike in an unexpected manner.
- Simplicity of planning is crucial. Always prepare clear, uncomplicated plans and precise orders to ensure they are executed correctly.

Simply, uncomplicated communication executed in an unexpected manner is a way to interpret von Clausewitz's message. His lesson is that you should focus on a single point, develop a plan that is simple to execute, and always look for ways to do the unexpected. Just like Sun Tzu's work, von Clausewitz favored the simple, cohesive, and unexpected. All of these attributes can be applied to effective brand communication strategy.

Now, let's fast-forward to more recent times. The lessons of these two great military strategists are continually being remade in business and marketing/advertising literature. Here are some key tenets from *Marketing Warfare* by Al Ries and Jack Trout (1983), *Strategy* by Michael E. Porter (1998), *Blue Ocean Strategy* by W. Chan Kim and Renée Mauborgne (2005) and *Good Strategy, Bad Strategy* by Richard Rumelt (2011):

- It's best to be first.
- Good strategy is unexpected.
- Make the competition irrelevant.
- Power your strengths.

Do these sound familiar? They should. All of these authors have developed excellent frameworks for analyzing strategy and/or principles for applying strategy. Their work was shaped by those early works of Sun

Tzu, Carl von Clausewitz, and several others. In many regards, strategy is timeless. What changes are the circumstances and situations. Now that we have had a brief history lesson, let's apply these principles to integrated brand communication.

Defining Strategy for Brand Communication

The key lessons from the history of strategy are:

- A brand communication plan needs to be simple, focused, and cohesive.
- The execution of that plan needs to be cohesive yet have an element of surprise or something unexpected.
- The plan and the execution should provide the brand with a competitive advantage in the marketplace.

Just like any strategy, the brand communication strategy is a plan to achieve a long-term goal. That goal in most cases is some form of brand growth or equity. That growth and/or equity is gained largely by how the brand is differentiated in the market. Based on this, the following is our working definition for integrated brand communication strategy:

"Integrated brand communication strategy is a single-focused communication plan executed in a cohesive and sometimes unexpected way that provides the brand with a competitive advantage in the marketplace."

Now let's take a look at how to apply this definition and why it is so important to view communication from a brand standpoint.

The 360 Degree Brand Viewpoint

The place to start is with the brand itself. When some people talk about a brand, they are referring to symbols, such as the name, logo, slogan, and/ or design. Our viewpoint of a brand includes these concrete symbols plus the positioning, experiences, and associations attached to the brand. So, the brand (which can be a specific product, company, and/ or organization) is the embodiment of all these tangible and intangible assets.

The job of the brand manager and communication professionals is to leverage these assets to increase the brand's equity. To accomplish this, there are marketing as well as communication levers.

FIGURE 1.1
360 Brand Viewpoint

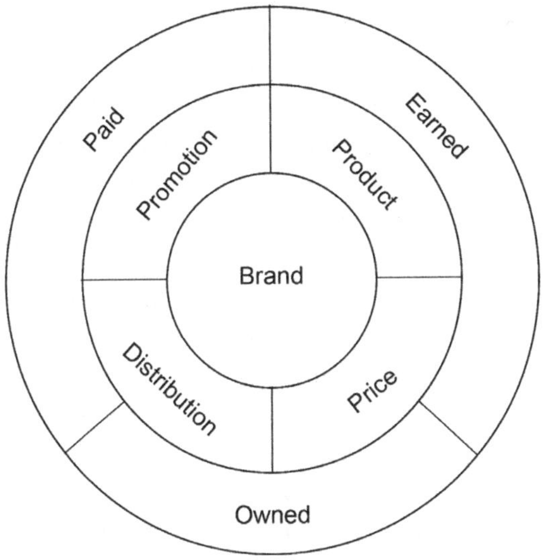

There are marketing and communication methods to unlock the brand's value. Marketing is the first ring that surrounds the brand. While there is a tendency to separate marketing decisions from communication decisions, our viewpoint is that every marketing decision impacts brand communication. There are four fundamental marketing buckets that impact the brand. Sometimes called the 4Ps, they include Product, Price, Place (distribution) and Promotion (includes communication):

- The brand is an outgrowth of the product itself. Brands begin with the product offering. The ingredients, the package, and the experience are all items that can enhance the brand's equity. Each of these items communicates something about the brand.
- Close to the product is price. How the brand is priced in the market makes a statement of its perceived value. Price and product form much of the brand's value proposition. Together they form a central aspect of brand communication.
- Next is distribution of the product. How do consumers find it and purchase it? Can it be purchased online, in a store, or both?

Is there an alternative distribution method? Where the brand is sold also makes a statement about its inherent value. If the brand is sold in a variety of channels, it may communicate convenience. If it is sold in only one place, it may communicate exclusivity.
- The final lever is promotion. This is how to incent the consumer to purchase the brand and to communicate its value. Promotion contains the way we communicate about the brand as well as how we may incentivize people to buy the brand. This is the bulwark of brand communication.

Each of these four areas offers strategic possibilities that we will cover in more detail in Chapter 2. The key point is that the strategies of each of these four areas must align to the brand. For example, if you are marketing a high-end watch, you may elect to keep your distribution channels scarce to reinforce the exclusive nature of the watch. Putting it in a mass merchandiser such as Walmart may go against the brand's position. The same is true of package design. A dated package design may communicate old fashioned when the brand needs to be contemporary. Or if the price is communicating cheap while your communication is saying quality, you may have consumer disconnect. Alignment of the 4Ps around the brand is crucial. They are the first part of integrated brand communication.

Brand communication is part of the fourth P, promotion. Promotion contains incentive, message, and media. Incentive is how to give the consumer a nudge to purchase the brand. If we are marketing a consumer package goods brand, a typical short-term incentive could be a short-term promotional offer such as buy one, get one free. An incentive doesn't have to be monetary. For example, TOMS Shoes offers a "buy one, give one" incentive where they provide a pair of shoes to children in need when you purchase a pair of their shoes. This is an example of giving back. And other brands develop messages about protecting the environment. Just like other elements of a brand, if incentives are used, they must align with the brand's positioning.

Message is the key aspect of the brand communication. What do you want to communicate about the brand? How will you do it? As we have discussed, a simple message executed in an unexpected way is the cornerstone to successful integrated brand communication.

Taken together, message and media form the basis for integrated brand communication. Just like marketing, brand communication surrounds the brand in three primary media forms: paid media, owned media, and earned media.

- Paid media is where the brand pays to be a part of a media channel. This could be a broadcast commercial or a paid search engine marketing campaign. Paid media is what most associate with integrated brand communication. This is outward brand communication designed to promote the brand. In this context, an integrated brand communication campaign is the cohesive coordination of paid media channels around a single-focused message. While this is a crucial aspect of brand communication, integrated brand communication contains so much more than a brand communication campaign.
- Owned media is the major area of brand communication growth in the past decade. Owned media is any media that is controlled by the brand. This could be the brand's website, Facebook page, Twitter feed, or YouTube channel. The rise of social media has been the catalyst for the growth of owned media. Unlike paid media, owned media offers the brand an opportunity to directly engage with its customers. This opportunity comes with a huge responsibility. Not only does the message and voice need to reflect the brand, the entire interaction experience needs to be consistent with the brand. And if the brand can be purchased through its website or social media, then that process also needs to be reflective of the brand. Owned assets are an extension of the brand. Since customers interact with the various owned media assets, there is a much greater opportunity for engagement and conversely, risk for poor engagement. Integrating owned media into the brand communication process is vital to the brand's ultimate success.
- Just like owned media, earned media is a great opportunity for the brand to extend its communication. Earned media is where media or customers become an unpaid media channel for the brand. Earned media has its roots in public relations. However, digital and social media have greatly enhanced the number of earned media opportunities not only for public relations

> professionals but for general customer brand conversations. Earned media has a tremendous upside for the brand. There is nothing better than an unpaid authentic endorsement of a brand coming from a customer. Conversely, there is nothing more damaging to a brand than customers or media that publish negative items about the brand. Managing the risk of earned media and folding it into the brand communication program is another brand communication opportunity.

Paid, owned, and earned communications are crucial for developing an integrated brand communication strategy. Together, the marketing wheel and communication wheel form the 360 degree brand communication viewpoint.

Summary

At its core, strategy is a plan with a purpose. Whether it is to conquer an enemy or to grow a brand, the fundamentals of strategy are consistent. One major lesson from the history of strategy is to develop a simple plan. From a military perspective, simple plans have a much higher likelihood of being correctly executed than a more complex plan. The same holds true in terms of brand communication. A simple message is much more likely resonate with the audience than a more complex message. Another important lesson is to ensure that your plan is cohesive. In the 360 degree brand communication viewpoint, there are a lot of moving pieces and parts. There are four marketing levers and three broad communication levers. Within each of these broad groups are a myriad of tactical items. Coordinating all the aspects of brand communication can become quite overwhelming . It is important to make sure that all the elements are working in concert to support the single focus of the brand's communication. The third lesson is that your plan needs to put the brand at a strategic advantage. Brands and communication both compete in the marketplace. The brand communication must not only be focused but it must also be meaningful. Developing communication that may be surprising or unexpected can be a way of gaining that strategic advantage.

In the next chapter, we are going to discuss how to build a strategic plan including the strategic opportunities available to brand communication and how they impact one another.

Review Questions

1. What are the three dictionary definitions of strategy?
2. What are the key lessons to be learned from the origins of strategy?
3. What is the definition of integrated brand communication strategy?
4. What are the components of the 360 degree view of brand strategy?

Discussion Questions

1. How would you define strategy?
2. How have the aspects of a brand communication plan changed over time?
3. What is similar and different about military strategy and brand communication strategy?
4. Is there a different set of criteria for evaluating brand communication strategy than other strategy?
5. Can you give an example of a brand that has a cohesive communication strategy? Can you give an example of a brand that doesn't have a cohesive communication strategy?

Additional Resources

Freedman, L. 2013. *Strategy: A History*. New York: Oxford University Press.

Keesee, Michael and Ankesh Kothari. 2010. *Strategy Daddy: Marketing Strategies, Tactics and Case Studies That Can Change the Competitive Landscape of Your Business*. Bellingham, WA: Parapet Press.

Kim, W. Chen and Renee Mauborge. 2005. *Blue Ocean Strategy: How to Create Uncontested Market Space and Make Competition Irrelevant*. Cambridge, MA: Harvard Business School Press.

Ohmae, Kenichi. 1982. *The Mind of the Strategist: The Art of Japanese Business*. New York: McGraw-Hill.

Porter, Michael. 1998. *Competitive Strategy: Techniques for Analyzing Industries and Competition*. New York: Free Press.

Ries, Al and J. Trout. 1983. *Marketing Warfare*. New York: McGraw-Hill.

Rumelt, R. 2011. *Good Strategy Bad Strategy: The Difference and Why It Matters*. New York: Random House.
Tzu, Sun. 2003. *The Art of War*. Translated from the Chinese edition by Lionel Giles, New York: Barnes and Noble.

Chapter 2

Components of Integrated Brand Communication Strategy

Learning Objectives

This chapter is intended to help you:

- Understand the dynamics of integrated brand communication
- Understand the connection of integrated brand communication
- Understand the components of integrated brand communication strategy
- Understand the Promotion versus Protection aspect of integrated brand communication

The Dynamics of a Brand

Just like people, brands are constantly evolving. They are not stagnant. Or if they are, they won't last long in the marketplace. And like a person, brands are multilayered. Brands are formed by experiences, associations, and communication. Brands move through their life accumulating experiences and associations that help define them. Brand communication reflects various layers of the brand.

A brand starts as either a product or a company. Every product or company was originally developed to meet a marketplace need. The founder(s) may have observed something about the business category or found an unmet consumer need. For example, State Farm Insurance began in 1922 with the simple idea that farmers should pay less for their auto insurance. The reason was that farmers drove fewer miles and had fewer accidents than those who lived in a city. It just seemed to be the fair thing to do. The idea of fairness helped propel State Farm Insurance to the number one insurance company in the United States.

Or take the case of Tide laundry detergent, which was developed in 1946. Tide was the original laundry detergent made especially for heavy-duty washing machines. The synthetic nature of Tide detergent was engineered for these "new" machines and was a significant improvement over regular laundry soap. Tide fulfilled a need in the marketplace just like State Farm. Like all successful brands, Tide and State Farm have constantly evolved to meet new needs.

The point is that brands start with an idea that changes the way you may think about a product category. In some cases, the brand may create a new category. Over time, these brands evolve. They add new features or product extensions to their origin brand. State Farm Insurance started with auto insurance and now offers life insurance, renters insurance, motorcycle, and boat insurance. It has even added banking services to its product mix. Tide started as a granular laundry detergent; over time it has added bleaching agents, softeners, and has even changed its form to be an encased capsule or what they call a POD.

Brands do evolve. And the consumer evolves as well. Consumer habits, values, and behavior change over time. This forces brands to change and evolve. For example, it is pretty clear that baby diapers are a product that is predominantly purchased by the baby's mother. Procter and Gamble introduced Pampers in 1961 when approximately 20 percent of women worked full-time. Today, over 60 percent of women work full-time. In the 1960s, it was rare that a mother was single. Today, well over 30 percent of mothers are single. Interestingly, according to a Pew research study, mothers in the 1960s spent 10 hours a day on average with their children while today's mother spends nearly 14 hours a day. So, today's mom now spends more time with her child even though she spends more time working outside the home. Pampers was initially introduced as an alternative to washing a cloth diaper in the 1960s. Today, Pampers is positioned as a brand that allows moms more time to spend with their children. From 1960 to now, Pampers is fundamentally the same product. Yet, it responds to vastly different times, which greatly impacts how it is communicated to its core audience.

Other outside forces can also impact the brand. Competition, legislation, social, and demographic changes all impact the brand. Just like we have seen with cultural trends, there are always outside influences that must be accounted for when developing a brand destination. For example, the consumer soft drink or CSD market is under serious scrutiny by the U.S. government. Soft drinks are viewed as a key contributor to our nation's obesity epidemic. As a result, there is a rapid movement to rid public schools of their soft drink machines. Many schools are replacing their favorite sodas with water or juice. In response to this growing discontent with the CSD industry, brands such as Coke are stepping up their communication to encourage young adults to be more active. They are working to be seen as a brand helping to provide a solution rather than as the problem.

Business consultants say that you can let change happen or you can make change happen. Brands that let change happen are in a reactionary position. They are less likely to control their brand's fate. To gain control, brands should constantly assess the forces that shape our society and get ahead of the curve. Understanding these forces forms the basis for using brand communication to help make the brand relevant.

Brand Destination Planning

As a brand strategist, you need to take charge of what direction you want the brand to go. You can't let it drift aimlessly. You need to figure out where you are going and how to best to get there. In other words, you need to define the destination.

Every day, you see brands that are responding to short-term pressures with no long-term vision. If you keep producing communication that just responds to today, you will likely end up with little long-term brand value. To produce a brand campaign, you need to step back and do some brand planning. You can't develop one without the other. Brand destination planning is one method to accomplish that task. It is built on some simple yet thought-provoking questions:

- Where are we today?
- Where do we want to be?
- How can we get there?

The answers to these questions establish the foundation for the strategic planning process. To answer these questions requires research that ultimately leads to insight.

To answer the initial question, "Where are we today?" you need to understand the brand's history. You also need to understand the brand's strengths and weaknesses. You then need to comprehend the consumer dynamics of the brand. You want to know what people think about your brand, how they buy the brand and why they buy the brand. This forms a picture of where the brand is in the consumer's mind. Brand perception leads to brand behavior. Through research you can better understand the barriers to why people may not be buying your brand or why people aren't buying your brand *more often*.

Based on understanding these barriers, you should begin to craft a vision for the brand that can expand the consumer's brand viewpoint. For example, Gatorade was developed to help hydrate athletes. It was a tremendous success. Success typically spawns imitators. Gatorade was no exception. Competitors began to claim this same ground and Gatorade began losing its differentiation. So, Gatorade conducted in-depth research regarding how athletes prepare for competition. What they found was that athletes had preparation rituals before, during, and after competition. Based on this insight, Gatorade reformulated the brand to meet these three different occasions. Gatorade changed from a sports drink company to a nutrition company. That was their brand destination.

A future vision of the brand doesn't always require a product improvement or change. It does require the brand find an insight that is compelling. Then it is up to the brand to use this insight to drive a future vision for the brand. For example, Pepto-Bismol updated its brand perception by changing how it aligned with consumer's needs. For years, Pepto-Bismol was viewed as a medicine to help you recover from an upset stomach. It became a medicine of last resort and was associated with sickness. Pepto-Bismol changed their approach from aligning with the outcome to aligning with the cause. The cause was overindulgence. Pepto-Bismol began telling consumers not to worry if they overdid it. Pepto-Bismol would be there to support them. This simple change in brand direction and communication helped Pepto-Bismol become a more relevant part of the consumer's life.

The 3 I's of Integrated Brand Communication Strategy

Integrated brand communication strategy consists of three I's: Insight, Idea, and Integration. Together they form the basis for and execution of the brand communication strategy. We just discussed how important it is to find an insight. An insight provides the foundation for building effective communication. We will delve more deeply into how to find an insight later in this book. Suffice it to say, a compelling insight is the cornerstone to great communication.

The same can be said of the second I: idea. Notice we said, the idea and *not* ideas. Just as we learned in Chapter 1, effective brand communication needs to be focused. The idea needs to be crystal clear. It should be so simple that you can phrase it in a single, short sentence. In the Gatorade example, the idea Gatorade communicated was, "Gatorade fuels athletic performance before, during, and after." Now, that is a simple, clear message.

Figure 2.1
Integrated Communication Strategy

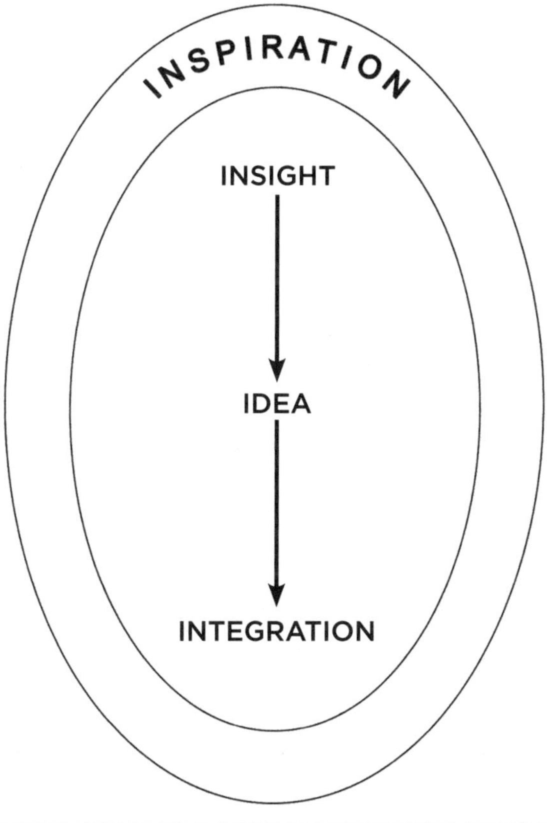

Integration is the final I. Proper integration requires that every facet of communication is focused on consistently delivering the idea. For brand communication to build brand equity, all communication elements must be aligned. This is not always the easiest task, with brands using a variety of communication partners. It is just human nature to want to put your own touch on the brand communication. Further complicating integration is the vast number of channels to coordinate. Together this puts a heavy burden on the execution of the brand communication strategy.

Figure 2.2
Components of an Integrated Brand Communication Strategy

1. Brand
   a. Brand Position
   b. Brand Destination
2. Situation Analysis
   a. SWOT
   b. Definition of Barriers
   c. Problem statement for brand communication
3. Insight
4. Strategic Idea
5. Target Market Strategy
6. Budget Strategy
7. Place and Timing Strategy
8. Communication Strategy
9. Creative Strategy
10. POE Media Strategy
11. Digital Strategy
12. Social Media Strategy
13. Brand Association
14. Promotional Strategy
15. Reputation Strategy
16. Evaluation Strategy

Components of Integrated Brand Communication

The components of an integrated brand communication strategy are highlighted in Figure 2.2.

As you can see, there are some key differences between an integrated brand communication strategy and just a communication strategy. Communication strategy is a subset of the former. An integrated brand communication strategy includes the following elements that are not usually part of communication strategy:

- The first difference is a clear definition of the brand and the plan to evolve the brand. While both brand positioning and brand destination can be baked into a communication strategy, here they form the foundation for all brand communication.
- The second key difference is a strategy for all aspects of the brand's communication including paid, earned, and owned media. Within this set of communication includes the brand's digital, social, association, and promotional strategies. For many brands, each of these elements may be developed by separate agencies of internal entities. In this case, it is all tied together in a single, seamless strategy.
- The third key difference is brand reputation management. A brand reputation management plan may reside outside the brand. It may be controlled or developed by a public affairs or corporate communication manager. Depending upon the brand and/or company, protecting the brand's reputation may be a corporate rather than a line management duty of the brand manager. In this case, we believe it is a key part of the integrated brand communication plan.

An integrated brand communication strategy contains items that are similar to any communication strategic plan. In the following chapters, we will be describing each of these elements and their strategic implications in detail. The following is a synopsis of each item beginning with the brand itself.

- The brand is at the core of all communication. Communication works to build the brand's equity. The stronger and more clearly defined the brand, the better the communication. We will be discussing what a brand is all about and the role that communication plays in brand equity in a later chapter.
- Like any strategic plan, the basis for building the plan begins with an assessment of the situation. Integrated brand communication strategy is no different. The situation analysis includes a SWOT (strengths, weaknesses, opportunities, and threats) analysis plus a definition of any barriers that may be impeding the desired destination of the brand. Included in this section is the problem statement defining the role of brand communication.
- The brand communication plan is built on an insight that can come from the consumer, the brand itself, the category, or category communication. This insight is crucial to the success of the communication since it represents the foundation that leads to the strategic idea. The strategic idea is the single focus that will move the brand in the desired direction. Together the insight and strategic idea are the linchpins to successful communication.
- The insight and strategic idea are tied to a clearly-defined target market. The target market strategy is a part of a three-legged strategic stool combined with the insight and strategic idea. The target market is the object of the idea with the intent of moving the target toward the brand. The most powerful insights typically come from the target market. It is linked to the insight and subsequent strategic idea.
- Budget is usually not thought of as a strategy, particularly in brand communication. It can be viewed as an outside corporate decision. However, budgeting is a crucial strategic element to the communication process. It dictates the type of approach and amount of activity that can be applied to the brand. Prior to tactical review of the plan, budget strategy is as important as other communication strategies.
- Where and when communication is to be delivered is a strategic component that sometimes doesn't get much attention.

Communication time and place, together with the much more heralded target market, form the three pillars to how communication will be ultimately delivered.

- Communication and creative strategy sound like the same thing but there are clear differences. Communication strategy is the overall strategy for the brand while creative strategy is the advertising or promotional message for the brand; they work hand in glove.
- Media strategy includes paid, earned, and owned media. It is the framework for how communication is delivered in the marketplace. The difference between a typical media plan and an integrated brand communication plan is that all aspects of communication are taken into consideration. Media planning historically has been predominantly about paid media. In this case, all digital media, social media, and brand associations as well as marketing public relations are a part of the integrated brand communication strategy.
- The promotional strategy is a part of the advertising/marketing strategy. In this case, we define promotional as a short-term sales incentive strategy. Promotional strategies must be in alignment with the brand as well as the communication and creative strategies.
- The brand reputation strategy is a crucial aspect of the brand communication strategy. Because this activity sometimes comes from corporate rather than brand, it is very important that messaging is aligned. This is particularly true of establishing a corporate or investor campaign that provides a halo for the brand. And, it is most important in a crisis situation where the brand needs to immediately act with integrity and authenticity.
- The final strategy is evaluation. Like budgeting, evaluation is not always seen as a strategy but rather a scorecard for measuring success. As we will discuss, how the brand sets into motion its evaluation process can greatly impact future brand communication.

There you have it. That is a brief synopsis of each element of the integrated brand communication strategy. They all work in concert to build brand equity. Each plays a crucial role in the ongoing brand communication. It is important to recognize that whether communication for promotion or protection, it all must be aligned to the brand.

Promotion and Protection

Most advertising textbooks and many brand managers focus their attention solely on communication that promotes the brand. This only makes sense since the goal of any brand is to gain more usage. The way to do that is to promote the brand either to gain consumer trial or to increase the number of uses among existing consumers.

The approach we advocate for integrated brand communication takes into account the protection of the brand as well as promotion. Protection of the brand and its communication involves a variety of issues and items. The first layer of brand communication protection is to ensure that the message, look, feel, and the meaning is consistent from one media channel to another. The second layer of protection is to ensure that outside forces are not taking the brand's message in an unwanted direction. For example, Twitter users railed against the 2015 resurrection of Colonel Sanders for KFC. This prompted the brand to quickly change out that specific spokesperson (the original Colonel) in favor of rotating a variety of Colonel Sanders spokespeople. And, the third layer of protection is to ensure that the brand is not damaged if there is some form of crisis. For example, Subway's long-term spokesman Jared Fogle's arrest for child pornography could have severely damaged the brand's reputation. Subway's rapid response by cutting ties with Fogle helped to mitigate this horrible event.

In today's rapid fire, social media world, it is crucial to keep an eye on both communication that promotes the brand as well as communication that protects the brand. Given that most brands have an active digital and social media program, this is even more vital today than ever before. A badly-worded tweet or an ill-advised post can quickly deteriorate into a crisis. Depending upon the severity, there can be long-term damage to the brand.

Summary

In summary, the components of an integrated brand communication strategy begin with the brand itself. They include the brand's position in the marketplace and the brand destination. Just like any plan, the first step is to develop a situation analysis. This is where you can assess the barriers to achieving the goal. For this you can define what role communication plays in solving the problem. The mid-section of an integrated communication strategic plan consists of an insight that is the basis for the strategic idea. The idea is designed to impact the brand's target market. Strategic decisions about budgeting, timing, creative, and media form the promotional aspect of the strategy. A reputation plan forms the protection aspect of the strategy. All of the strategies are set to specific measureable objectives. Each objective is constantly reevaluated so that communication can be fine-tuned.

Review Questions

1. What are the dynamics of brand communication?
2. What are the components of an integrated brand communication plan?
3. What are the three key Is that need to be aligned for a strategy to work in the marketplace?
4. What is the difference between brand promotion and brand protection?

Discussion Questions

1. How do advertising agencies outline their campaign plans? How does it compare to the integrated brand communications plan?
2. Who should be responsible for brand promotion and brand protection? Should it be an internal or external brand resource?
3. What are other examples of brands that have successfully developed an integrated brand communication campaign that connects an insight to an idea to a complete plan? Review WARC cases, EFFIE cases, and *Ad Age* for examples.

Additional Resources

Keesee, M. and A. Kothari. 2010. *Strategy Daddy: Marketing Strategies, Tactics and Case Studies That Can Change the Competitive Landscape of Your Business*. Bellingham, WA: Parapet Press.

Kelley, L. and D. Jugenheimer. 2015. *Advertising Account Planning: Planning and Managing an IMC Campaign*. New York: Routledge.

Mark, M. and C. Pearson. 2001. *The Hero and the Outlaw: Building Extraordinary Brands Through the Power of Archetypes*. Maidenhead, UK: McGraw-Hill.

Ries, A. and J. Trout. 2000. *Positioning: The Battle for Your Mind*. New York: McGraw-Hill.

Steel, J. 2006. *Perfect Pitch: The Art of Selling Ideas and Winning New Business*. Hoboken, NJ: Wiley.

Chapter 3

Defining the Brand and Role of Communication

Learning Objectives

This chapter is intended to help you:

- Understand brand properties
- Understand brand positioning
- Understand the essence of a brand
- Understand how to define the communication problem

Brand Properties

A brand is constantly evolving. Our goal with brand destination planning is to continue to move the brand in a relevant direction. Over time, experiences and associations become attached to a brand. In this way, brands are very similar to people. Both brands and people have properties that become attached to their persona. These are elements of what make you unique.

As you grow and mature, you gain more experiences and accumulate associations. Some of them you keep and some you shed. For example, you may want to keep the association with your college once you graduate. That may become important as you seek a job. On the other hand, that night your party went viral on YouTube may be something you are trying to distance yourself from.

A brand is also a collection of experiences and associations. The brand is a symbolic embodiment of all the information and properties connected to it. Brands have tangible and intangible properties. The most commonly known properties are the brand name, logo, slogan, and design. Brands can have many properties such as mascots, spokespeople and other associations, events, and brand experiences.

Figure 3.1
Brand Design Schematic

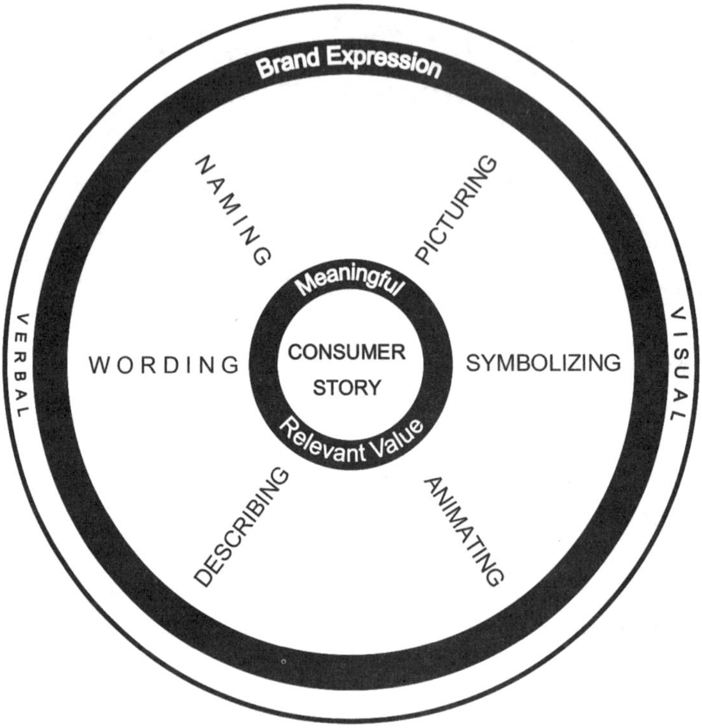

One way to make a brand more relevant is to add positive experiences and associations. On the flip side, there may be opportunities to subtract associations that are less relevant today than in the past. Either way, brand communication plays a huge role in the formulation and reformulation of the brand. How and what you communicate can add to or change the conversation about the brand. Just think of how you talk about yourself. That crazy party that made you a minor college celebrity when you were young is likely not something you talk about when you are a senior executive. Conversely, the college or school you graduated from could become a lifetime association.

In his book, *Building Strong Brands*, David Aaker developed a brand design schematic that demonstrates how a brand is comprised of various experiences and associations. Figure 3.1 shows the brand schematic template and Figure 3.2 provides an example of the brand schematic for McDonald's.

Figure 3.2
McDonald's Brand Design

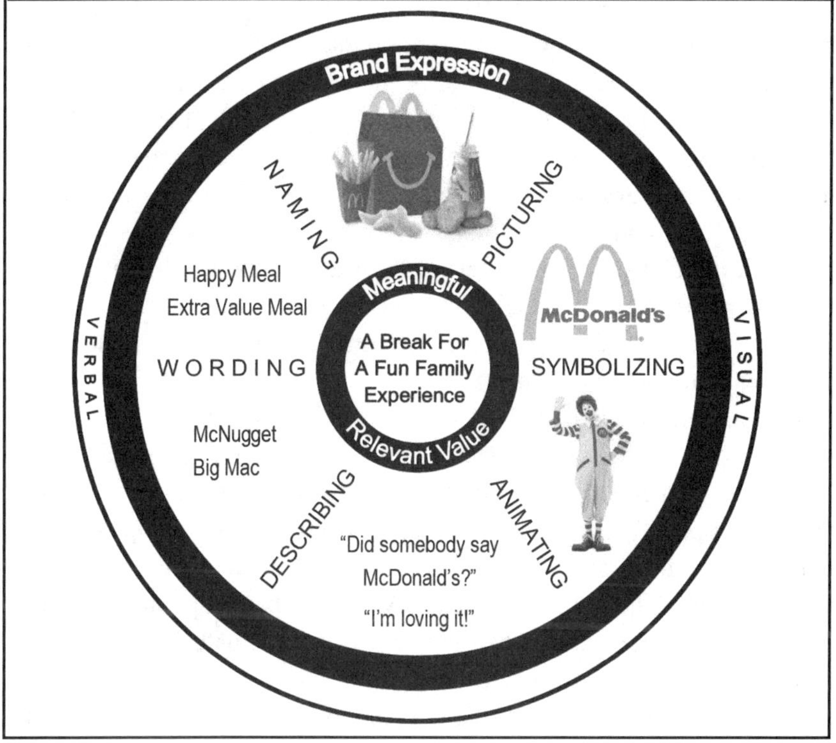

As you can see, there are verbal and visual brand expressions. McDonald's is an excellent example of how brand communication has become such a big part of its overall brand. There are very few brands that actually have a naming convention for their entire menu or product line. McDonald's has the "MAC" language which serves the brand very well. There is no question about what hamburger you are talking about if it is a Big Mac. Or if you are ordering Chicken McNuggets, you know exactly what brand is promoting it. The "Mac" language is a powerful asset for the brand. It is clearly identified with the brand and becomes a part of the consumer's lexicon.

Visually, McDonald's has the Golden Arches. This symbol is so powerful that McDonald's uses it without the name McDonald's to identify the restaurant. Other key symbols are the brand characters such as Ronald McDonald or the Hamburglar. And associations and experiences such as the Ronald McDonald House charity and the Ronald McDonald High

School All-American team portray the brand in a good light. They all are important brand properties.

Even iconic brands such as McDonald's add to and subtract from their brand. The Hamburglar, who has been on hiatus for the past fifteen years was recently updated and added back into the brand's mix. New music, "I'm loving it," has replaced such iconic songs as, "Did somebody say McDonald's?" and "You deserve a break today." And the brand has made its way into a more upscale concept with its McCafe style restaurant. McDonald's is constantly adding to and subtracting from its brand to maintain its relevance. It is a part of its strategy. By developing new or revitalizing established associations and experiences, brands such as McDonald's can not only stay in the consumer's consciousness but sometimes leap into popular culture.

Adding relevant associations and/or events to the brand is a cornerstone of great brand communication. By adding a vivid metaphor to the brand, you will enhance its value. Dos Equis was just another beer until they developed "The Most Interesting Man in the World" campaign. That helped propel the brand to new heights and it added another dimension to the brand. Now the "Most Interesting Man" is a part of popular culture.

Brand properties should be viewed as symbols of the brand and its position in the marketplace. Brand properties need to be strategically added to or deleted from the brand to support this position. It is not unlike a character in a story. That character needs to be well-defined. Brand positioning is to the brand what character development is to a play. The clearer the definition, the more powerful is the role.

Positioning the Brand

How the brand is positioned in the marketplace is a core strategic decision. Brand positioning can determine success and failure. If the brand isn't positioned properly, it will likely lack differentiation. Or if not properly positioned, it may lack an emotional connection with the target market.

To position a brand, you need to make a series of strategic decisions. Figure 3.3 is a brand positioning format that originated with Procter and Gamble. P&G is credited with the development of many brand management practices. This is one of the most important tools used in brand management.

While the elements of the brand position look simple enough, it is their interaction that makes this positioning tool so powerful. The first

Figure 3.3
Classic Positioning Statement

Brand Positioning Statement

To ________________, _______________ is the brand of
(TARGET MARKET) (BRAND)
__________________________ that ________________
(COMPETITIVE FRAMEWORK) (BENEFIT)
because _______________________________________
(REASON WHY)

The brand personality is _________________________.

element is a strategic decision we will discuss in greater detail later in this book. That is how to define the target market. The target audience is not just a demographic group. It should contain the target's mind-set or motivation. It is this mind-set or motivation that your brand is tapping into. If you are talking to "cash-strapped moms" versus "style-driven moms," you can quickly recognize that your brand needs to be positioned a bit differently to effectively address each target market.

The target market is the driving force behind the brand's position. It is the single most important element to creating effective brand communication. Understanding the target market is crucial to developing brand communication that can add value to the brand. The target market should be so clearly defined that it becomes like writing to one person.

The second element of the brand positioning statement is the frame of reference. This refers to the brand's competitive set. This may seem like a simple decision. If you are marketing Coke, isn't your frame of reference other carbonated soft drinks? Pepsi and Dr Pepper are among those in this category. Or as the category leader in carbonated soft drinks, do you consider a broader category such as any drink that quenches one's thirst? The industry terms this the liquid refreshment beverage category. This includes everything from tap water to milk, coffee, tea, fruit juice, energy drinks, bottled water, and carbonated soft drinks. It is basically anything that you drink. This opens up a whole new way of thinking.

Consider drinks with a high caffeine content such as Mountain Dew. This brand's frame of reference could extend to energy drinks and even coffee if you define the category as energy-boosting drinks.

Defining who you need to beat is clearly a strategic decision. It will impact how you position the brand. As you define the brand's position in the marketplace, it is important to look at it from a number of perspectives. The first is from the consumer's perspective. How do consumers view the various categories? Do they just pick a drink or do they consciously select from a more narrowly-defined category such as tea or carbonated soft drinks? The second perspective is how you would like the consumer to view the brand. Do you want to position your brand against a narrow category or a broader one? This requires a serious strategic discussion. Much of the definition of who you need to beat can be answered with the next two elements of the brand positioning statement. These are the brand benefit and the supporting reason why.

The brand benefit and supporting reason why form the basis for brand communication. The benefit is what the brand does for the consumer. And the reason why is the supporting evidence or feature/attribute. For example, having lower prices than any other store is a compelling attribute. The benefit is that consumers can buy more of what they want. For a benefit to be so distinctive that you cannot substitute another brand in its place requires a very compelling feature or attribute. Attributes/features and benefits work hand-in-glove. Benefits can be functional or emotional. Buying more of what you want is a functional benefit. It is what the brand's attribute or feature provides for the consumer. In this case, consumers can buy more. A functional benefit is not what a consumer feels. That is an emotional benefit. In this example, buying more can mean living better or providing better for your family or being a smart and savvy shopper. Hitting a consumer's emotional hot button is the goal of every brand.

Strategically, you position a brand so that it is distinctive. That can be based on a functional benefit or an emotional benefit. We will discuss this in much more detail later in this book. Many brands begin their positioning based on communicating a functional benefit. This is where most brands begin—they form their business based on a compelling feature or attribute that offers the consumer a benefit. As the competition either copies or imitates this feature, the brand may need to move to claim an emotional position in the category.

Capturing an emotional position in the category can be very powerful.

Would you rather sell inexpensive goods or sell living better? Coke has built its powerhouse brand position on creating happiness. That is much stronger than providing a refreshing drink. Like most brands, even Coke evolved from a brand that talked about "Refreshing Taste" to a brand that talked about "Have a Coke and a Smile" to "Open Happiness." Each aspect of Coke's communication built upon the other. Without having a refreshing taste, Coke couldn't claim the emotional ground of "happiness." Each aspect of the brand needs to support the overall position. The strategy in working through what benefit the brand can own is a crucial part of any brand's success.

Brand Essence

Brand essence is the long-term emotional position of the brand. Unlike brand communication that is constantly evolving and changing, a brand's essence should remain largely unchanged. It is a foundational element of the brand. Communicating that brand essence is extremely important to the overall strategy for the brand. Brand essence is typically summed up in either a sentence or in just a few words.

For example, Coke exists as a brand to create happiness in everyday life. Coke's brand essence is "refreshing happiness." The Coke brand philosophy is that of "liquid and linked." It is about sharing happiness. This leads to creating brand experiences focusing on happiness that can become stories that move from the brand to its people, from people to people, and from people back to the brand.

Brand essence is complimentary to brand positioning. A brand is initially positioned in the market based on a unique set of features that translate to a consumer benefit. This functional benefit can be leveraged into an emotional benefit. The brand essence represents that core emotional benefit. It should be something that the brand stands for. The brand expression or brand essence is the "meaningful relevant value" of the brand, as noted earlier by David Aaker. The brand essence is typically used internally by the company to describe the brand. It may or may not be expressed externally.

Nike's brand essence, "Authentic Athletic Performance," is a great example of a strictly internal brand expression. Nike doesn't use "authentic athletic performance" in any of its outward facing brand communication. "Just do it" has been their tagline for many years. However, Nike does use "authentic athletic performance" as the brand standard for everything they do. All of their communication reflects this brand essence and all of their brand associations reflect this as well. Nike lives their brand essence. If something isn't authentic, then it doesn't fit the brand. Think about all the communication that Nike does. It is all actual athletic feats. Some are incredible, yet they all are credible. That is the point. The brand essence should be more than just a few words on a page. It should become the brand standard for all brand activity.

There is likely not a better two words that capture the long-term emotional position of a brand as "Caring Shared" does for Hallmark. Those simple two words capture the emotional nature of Hallmark's business. They provide a platform for all of Hallmark's brand activity no matter the type of message or type of medium. No matter if it is a Hallmark card or a digital message or even a television program, any content can be applied to this umbrella thought.

A brand's essence then becomes shorthand for describing the brand. Rather than providing a complete brand positioning statement, the brand essence summarizes it in a few words. A strong brand essence such as the examples we discussed help strategically frame the brand. The brand essence provides a navigational star for all of the brand's activity. It becomes the sole for any future brand communication.

Defining the Communication Problem

In every business, there are problems. Or, you can frame them as opportunities or challenges. Regardless of the semantics, every business or brand faces obstacles in their quest to grow. From a business standpoint, growth may mean increasing market share or sales. From a financial perspective, growth may be to increase margin and/or bottom-line revenue. There are typically barriers in the way of achieving these growth objectives.

The question is, "Can communications solve the problem?" Not every brand problem can be solved using communications. Defining the problem and the role that communication may play in solving that problem is crucial. This is the highest-level strategic communication question. The key aspect to defining the problem is that of defining the role that communication may play in the solution.

Communication may play a big role in solving the problem. It may be a part of the answer to solving a problem or it may not be the answer at all. Let's take a look at an example of each scenario.

- If the brand problem is a lack of awareness, then that is a problem that communication will play a huge role in solving.

Raising awareness is one of the top benefits of a strong outward facing communication program.

- If the brand problem is a lack of distribution, then communication may be a part of the solution but not the total solution. Imagine that your brand is a new condiment. The challenge is to gain grocery distribution. The brand's sales team needs to convince the grocery buyer to carry the item. The brand sales team may request that there be a communication plan that features this grocer as a part of their sell-in package. Communication is not the total answer to getting the brand on the grocer's shelf. However, it is an important ingredient in the overall sales effort.
- If the brand problem is with the product itself, there may be little that communication can do. If the brand has a defect or flaw that is keeping consumers from purchasing it, communication is not the answer. The answer is to fix the brand first before communicating. In this situation, one of the worst actions a brand manager can take is to communicate before the problem is corrected. That will lead to more consumers trying a flawed brand. The result could be a rapid demise for the brand.

Communication is a tremendous asset in solving certain problems. We mentioned awareness as one area where communication can play a large role. The following are some other key problem areas including awareness where communication can play a large role in the solution.

- When the problem is to increase awareness.
- When the problem is to change attitudes or perceptions.
- When the problem is to convey something new.
- When the problem is to update or change a brand image.
- When the problem is to protect the brand's image or reputation.

From a business standpoint, communication can play a big role in helping a brand gain consumer trial and/or repeat purchase. Communication can convey the benefits of the brand or the program to accelerate repeat purchase. Communication can also play a big role in helping a brand's margin through keen differentiation. For luxury goods, communication plays a central role in helping the brand to maintain a premium price. Communication can help bring associations to the brand that help bolster its quality image.

Clearly defining the problem and the role that communication may play in solving the problem is a core strategic decision. A fuzzy problem may result in the misapplication of communication. Then the problem is not solved. Worse yet for the brand communicator, communication is seen as a strategy that won't work. Like any strategy, communication will only work well when it is solving a problem in its wheelhouse. It is incumbent upon the brand communication team to ensure that the first part of the communication process is to clearly define the problem.

Summary

In summary, a brand is a collection of associations and experiences. Brand communication is focused on making those associations and experiences relevant. As the consumer evolves, so must the brand and brand communication. Adding brand properties or subtracting properties may be necessary to maintain relevancy. Brand positioning is a framework for maintaining differentiation in the marketplace. A brand positioning statement contains a series of interrelated strategic decisions. Those include defining the target market, the competitive set, and the brand's unique benefit that is evidence-based. The more compelling the evidence, the stronger the brand's differentiation. Brand essence is the long-term core emotional position of the brand. It is normally summed up in a sentence or a couple of key words. The brand essence is used as internal shorthand for what the brand stands for. A strong brand essence becomes the standard for all brand activity. The role that brand communication plays in solving brand growth problems depends upon the problem. Not every brand growth problem can be solved using brand communication. Brand communication is most often used to solve issues such as a lack of awareness or to help change a consumer attitude or perception. Brand communication can be an important part of other growth barriers such as gaining more distribution or helping to support a brand's pricing stance. Brand communication is an important asset in the brand toolkit. As any tool, it must be used to solve the right problem.

Review Questions

1. How do brands add or subtract properties from themselves? When should a brand consider subtracting an established property from itself?

2. How does brand positioning work? Does positioning always relate directly to the brand benefit and attribute?
3. What are the differences between an attribute and a benefit?
4. What is a brand essence? How is it different than a brand position?

Discussion Questions

1. Analyze a brand based on Aaker's brand schematic. What brand properties does it contain? Where would be opportunities for additions? Should a property be updated or subtracted?
2. Analyze a brand positioning statement. Now compare it to its brand essence. What are the similarities? Are there any differences?
3. How do people position themselves? How do politicians position themselves? How is personal positioning different than brand positioning?
4. What is your brand essence? Can you sum up yourself in a sentence or a few words?
5. Can you think of other examples where brand communication won't solve a brand's problem? Are there different problems that are better solved by advertising than public relations or vice versa?

Additional Resources

Aaker, D. 2011. *Building Strong Brands*. New York: Free Press.

Bedbury, S. and S. Fenichell. 2003. *A New Brand World: Eight Principles for Achieving Brand Leadership in the Twenty-first Century*. Middlesex, UK: Penguin.

Bly, Robert W. 2006. *The Copywriter's Handbook: A Step-By Step Guide to Writing Copy That Sells*. 3rd ed. New York: Henry Holt and Company.

Kelley, L. and D. Jugenheimer. 2015. *Advertising Account Planning: Planning and Managing an IMC Campaign,* 3rd ed. New York: Routledge.

Ries, A. and L. Ries. *The 22 Immutable Laws of Branding: How to Build a Product or Service into a World Class Brand*. New York: HarperCollins.

Ries, A. and J. Trout. 2000. *Positioning: A Battle for Your Mind*. New York: McGraw-Hill.

Chapter 4

Budget Strategy

Learning Objectives

This chapter is intended to help you:

- Understand the components of a brand communication budget
- Learn strategic budgeting approaches
- Understand the difference between fixed and variable budget items
- Understand the financial implications of a budget

Brand Communication Budget Components

One of the biggest questions facing any brand is how many dollars should be devoted to brand communication? That question may elicit many different answers and opinions depending upon your perspective.

A brand manager may believe that brand communication is underspent. A chief financial officer may believe that it is overspent. And a CEO may think that neither the brand manager nor CFO understand how best to optimize brand communication spending. Like so many monetary decisions, there are lots of opinions yet few absolute answers.

A good place to start with brand communication budgeting is to identify what compromises the budget. Figure 4.1 provides budget categories for a typical consumer brand. The budget categories are organized into three broad areas: working budget, nonworking budget and overhead and fees.

Items that provide brand exposure are many times referred to as the working budget. This is the money allocated to provide brand exposure. Paid media, events and sponsorships and promotional items/collateral are standard budget line items for this category.

Non-working budget items are production, research and perhaps a contingency fund. These are all items that are important to the communication process but are not viewed by the consumer.

The final category is overhead and fees. This includes personnel, agency and other suppliers' fees as well as software or subscriptions. This budget category is dollars that form the foundation for development of the brand communication program.

Let's begin by evaluating the working budget.

Figure 4.1
Communication Budget Categories

Budget Categories

Working Budget

- Paid Media
- Events and Sponsorships
- Promotional Items/Collateral
- Owned Media

Non-working Budget

- Production
- Research
- Contingency

Overhead and Fees

- Agency Fees (Advertising, Digital, Public Relations, Specialty)
- Internal Salaries/Freelancers
- Design Fees
- Software and Subscriptions

Working Budget

The first component under the working budget header is what is typically associated with brand communication. That is paid media advertising. When most people discuss brand communication budgeting, the first item that is usually on the list is advertising spending. Since paid media can be very costly, we know that the budget will dictate the brand's media communication channels. For example, if the brand has a $2 million budget, placing a $5.0 million 30 second television commercial in the Super Bowl is out of the question. One Super Bowl commercial is more than twice the amount of the brand's total budget. Paid media is a key consideration for any brand communication program. The budget will greatly impact the strategic brand communication decisions that can be made.

Just like paid media, events and sponsorships help put the brand front and center with its audience. Many brands use events and/or sponsorships to gain a positive brand association. If you are marketing an auto accessory, then a tie-in with NASCAR may make sense. Or, if you are in charge of recruiting for the Navy, the X Games are a great venue to promote your brand.

Sponsorships and events have some key differences from paid media. Sponsorships and events typically contain a media component. However, that is just part of the cost. Most sponsorships bundle into their costs, tickets, promotional mentions, possible promotions/give-aways and exclusive rights. Plus there can be additional costs to activate promotions that may require personal interaction with consumers.

Promotional items and collateral material can compromise a part of a working budget. These two categories may be used primarily to support the sales organization. However, they can have broader usage. For example, promotional items can range from pens and coffee mugs to expensive luggage or even airline tickets. Promotional items can be a part of a consumer promotional event or they may be used as a leave behind for the sales organization.

Collateral material can be as simple as a printed sales sheet for the sales organization or as complex as a digital brochure. For example, if you are working on an automotive brand, then you may be developing printed materials to support the brand at the dealership and a digital brochure to support the brand on a national basis.

Owned media is a relatively new budget category. This typically includes the brand's website and social media properties. In today's communication landscape, most brands have some form of social media presence. This could be a Facebook or Twitter account. Or the brand may extend into more social media platforms such as LinkedIn, Pinterest, Instagram and Tumblr. Regardless, there is a cost to updating these assets. Owned media can extend to many other items that the brand may control including brand created events or other media properties.

The strategic goal in budgeting is to ensure that the working budget represents the highest percentage of budget dollars. Seventy percent or more of the total brand dollars spent should be applied to the working budget.

Non-working Budget

Non-working budget items are those that are not visible to the consumer yet are important to the overall brand communication program.

The largest item in this category typically is production. This is the cost to produce all the communication content. Under this heading may be video, audio, print and digital production. Some of this work may be done in-house. Other production needs may include hiring a specific company to direct and produce content such as broadcast commercials or films.

Within the production category, there are likely to be sub-categories that itemize the steps or costs within each production job. For example, in developing a television commercial, there will likely be a line item for the director, talent, and post production and location fees. Each production job can become complex. Production can become costly, particularly if you are producing high end video commercials or films. It is not unusual for those jobs to run in the hundreds of thousands of dollars. Sometimes television commercials can cost over a million dollars.

Production costs vary considerably depending upon the brand. Some brands have a high need for constant content. Others do not. Production costs may be very high when developing a new campaign and low once that campaign is in the market. As a result, production budgets largely range from 10 percent to 20 percent of the total communication budget.

Most brand communication programs contain research. Research may be used to track the program's success. Research can also be used to help guide the development of creative content. Typically research is conducted by a third party research supplier that focuses on communication research.

Research costs also vary depending upon the phase of the brand communication program. Like production, research costs are higher when launching a new campaign than when just measuring an existing effort. Research costs are typically between less than 1 percent to upwards of 5 percent of the total brand communication budget.

The last line item in the non-working budget category is the contingency fund. Contingency funds are dollars set aside for various uses. One use may be to cover unexpected expenses or overages. Another use may be for opportunistic purchases of media. Brands usually set aside between 1 percent to 3 percent of their budget in some form of contingency fund.

Strategically, the goal of budgeting for non-working dollars is to use caution so that you can apply the greatest percent of your budget to working dollars. Some brand communication managers develop a new campaign at the end of one budget year so that they can launch it with new dollars in the subsequent year. This tactical approach can maximize the impact of the available budget.

Overhead and Fees

Overhead and fees are those items that apply to salaries, software, subscriptions and agency compensation. When developing a communication budget, these are important corporate items.

Agency fees are likely to be the largest portion of this budget category. Depending upon the brand, you may work with a full service agency or separate creative and media agencies. There are lots of specialty agencies such as public relations or digital specialists that may also be on your agency roster. There are also niche agencies that may provide specialized services such as consumer promotions, trade show support or search engine marketing.

Advertising agencies used to be compensated based on some form of media commission. The early industry standard was 15 percent. Now, that number can be much lower depending upon the size of the paid media budget. With the advent of media agencies, there are fewer full service agencies, meaning that an ad agency may just be doing strategy and creative execution. As a result, agencies are largely compensated based on some form of fee.

Fees are usually tied to the number of hours worked on the brand's account plus an overhead factor. For example, if the agency estimates that it might take 3000 hours to support the client at an average hourly rate of $90 per hour, then hourly fee is pegged at $270,000. This fee is multiplied by some form of overhead factor that ranges from 1.75 to 2.25. So, if the overhead in this example is 2.0, then the agency fee (hourly rate x 2 overhead factor) would be $540,000. This fee would provide the agency with the necessary compensation to apply the appropriate personnel to the brand for a full year.

There are lots of different agency compensation models. Some have a base fee plus a performance bonus based on agreed upon metrics. Other forms include a sliding commission scale with the more the advertiser spends, the less the commission percentage.

Then there are compensation models that are tied to how much profit the agency makes on an account. A recognized cap such as 15 percent or 20 percent is agreed upon. The advertiser then audits the agency to make sure this is not exceeded.

The strategic point of agency compensation is to ensure that both parties are fairly treated. As an advertiser, you want the most from your agency. That means paying them to make a fair profit. On the other side, you want to make sure that you don't pay more than necessary. So, agency compensation does become quite a balancing act.

The other personnel budget items under overhead and fees column include internal salaries plus any freelance and design work. Depending upon the brand's needs, there may be a department or just a few people internally devoted to brand communication. If brand communication is ongoing, then it may make sense for the brand to consider bringing that activity in-house rather than using an outside agency. The trend for brands that have a considerable amount of owned media is to have an internal staff that handles that activity. There are also administrative duties and other coordination duties that require internal personnel.

One way to gain staffing flexibility is to hire freelance or contract workers. If the brand has an annual event that requires work for just a few months, then it may make more sense to hire a contract worker for that time rather than commit to a fulltime employee. Freelancers can be helpful in terms of content development or as strategic counsel.

In Figure 4.1, we isolated design fees as a special budget category. If a brand requires a new packaging design, logo or industrial design, that requires a specialized design firm. Design may be a single project or it can be an ongoing process. It is usually separate from other agency fees.

Brand communication requires budgeting for software needs and subscriptions. Software needs may include a license fee or just an outright purchase. For example, you may purchase Adobe creative suite for graphic needs or software to help manage the website. Subscriptions may be items such as social media monitoring services or just trade publication subscriptions. All of these are costs that require prior budgeting.

Figure 4.2
Communication Budget Strategic Approaches
Pros and Cons

Method

1. **Percent of Sales**
    a. Pros: Simple. Can be used to benchmark competition.
    b. Cons: Backward looking. May not reflect communication needs.
2. **Objective/Task**
    a. Pros: Forward looking.
    b. Cons: Difficult to know if dollars will achieve the task
3. **Competitive Share of Spending**
    a. Pros: Pegs spending to potential market share growth
    b. Cons: Backward looking. Competition may change.
4. **All you can afford**
    a. Pros: Simple. Use to prioritize tasks.
    b. Cons: Lacks strategic focus
5. **Return on Investment Simulation**
    a. Pros: Ultimate decision strategy.
    b. Cons: Very difficult to predict.
6. **Continual Testing**
    a. Pros: Offers constant in market evaluation
    b. Cons: Difficult to understand how to react.

Strategic Budget Approaches

Now that we understand a bit more about what comprises a budget, let's discuss how to determine the budget. There are a number of strategic approaches.

Figure 4.2 outlines six different strategic budget approaches including the pros and cons for each. Let's examine how each budget strategy plays out.

Percent of Sales

One method of developing a brand communication budget is to determine a percent of brand sales that is devoted to communication. For example, if you determine that you should allocate 3 percent of the total brand's sales of $100 million to communication, then the budget would be $3 million.

The benefit of this approach is that it is simple. All you have to do is one simple calculation and you have the budget. It also works well with an overall corporate budgeting allocation process where funds are allocated as a percent of revenue.

Strategically, this approach can be used to benchmark the competition. Competitive brand communication spending plus their respective revenue can be used to compare each brand's percent of sales devoted to communication.

For example, let's assume that you are in charge of the brand that competes in the liquid refreshment beverage category. Your brand has allocated 5 percent of its revenue to communication in the past yet the category has allocated 8 percent. You know that in this upcoming year, there will be new competitive brands entering the marketplace. In this case, allocating a greater percent of revenue dollars for communication may be a strategically sound move.

The Percent of Sales method works well when your brand is mature and the category you compete in is also mature. Since there are a lot of brands and categories that fit this definition in the United States, this method is popular.

When your brand is new or the category is undergoing significant change, this method falls down. It is a backward-looking method. You are assessing the past performance of your brand and other brands. The other brands may elect to change their strategy which could impact your assumptions. This method also may not reflect the communication needs of your brand.

Objective/Task

The Objective/Task method for budgeting requires you to correlate your communication objectives with a desired outcome. In theory, this is a terrific budget model. For example, if you have correlated the reach and frequency of your communication plan with awareness, attitude, and usage impact of the consumer, you have a very powerful tool. This requires some very strong research to develop a model that can be a trusted future forecast.

The Objective/Task method is used for new products that don't have a track record. By estimating the communication needs that will drive business goals, you can build a budget model. This is easier said than done.

Strategically, this method is excellent for assessing the impact of various levels of communication support. You can develop "what if" scenarios that require different budget commitments. Ultimately, your goal is to develop the best communication plan that will meet the goal.

Competitive Share of Spending

Trying to beat the competition is an ongoing goal for any brand. Few brands have the luxury of being a monopoly or competing in an oligopoly. One approach to developing a budget is to peg your brand's spending to the other brands in the category relative to market share.

This spending approach is termed Share of Spending/Share of Market or SOS/SOM. This analysis compares the share of the brand's spending in the category to that of its market share. For example, suppose your brand spent $5 million last year on communication, with the total category spending $50 million. Your brand would have spent 10 percent of the category or a 10 percent SOS. If you then compare that to your brand's market share, 10 percent, then the brand is spending in line with its market share or SOM.

Research suggests that to grow a brand's market share requires investing at a higher level in communication than that of its market share. For example, if we increased our brand spending from $5 million to $10 million and the category remained constant at $50 million, then the brand's

SOS would be 20 percent. This is twice the level of its 10 percent market share. This indicates that the brand is aggressive about attaining growth.

Conversely, if the brand adjusted its spending down to $2.5 million, its SOS would be 5 percent. This indicates that the brand is not aggressive about growing market share through the use of brand communication.

This strategic approach is based upon a large body of research suggesting brands that invest in brand communication at a higher rate than their market share will be more likely to see market share growth than those brands that do not.

The benefit of this approach is that it pegs spending toward an anticipated growth in market share. This provides the brand with a return on investment analysis. By forecasting a spending percentage and market share percentage, a brand can estimate what market share it may be able to attain with all other factors being constant.

The latter is the downside of the equation. It is difficult to forecast what the competition may do. Brand communication in the category may remain the same or it may accelerate at a rapid rate. It can be difficult to forecast. In mature categories, this approach may be easier to forecast since there is a long track record of spending. In high growth or new categories, this may become more difficult.

All You Can Afford

So, what will it take to get the results you need? I don't know, what do you have? This is the essence of the All You Can Afford method of budgeting. Before dismissing this budget method entirely, there are some strong benefits for this method.

First off, it is simple. You know what you have to spend. Second, just knowing the limitations of your spending helps prioritize what you can accomplish. Third, it makes you innovate so that you can get more dollars next year.

If management has indicated that either this percentage of revenue or absolute dollar amount is all that can be afforded, then it is your job to make the most of it. That is perhaps the simple beauty of this method. It takes the pressure off on wondering if you should have more or less dollars. You know what you have and you make the most of what you've got.

This budget strategy is popular with new brands where you decide how much is affordable. As a brand gets a track record, this method becomes less strategic since with more brand revenue, comes more flexibility in terms of budgeting.

Return on Investment Simulation

This is the holy grail of budgeting. Everyone wants to know what your return on investment will be. If you can demonstrate that for every dollar invested you will return five dollars, then it is likely that you will get the budget you desire.

Developing a return on investment model is easier said than done. The marketing mix is complex. Isolating the effect that communication alone has on sales is not easy. However, it can be done. There are literally hundreds of case studies from the World Advertising Research Council (WARC) that demonstrate the effect of communication on sales.

In today's data driven world, there are more opportunities than ever to develop a predictive model for your brand. It takes ongoing tracking of sales coupled with ongoing tracking of communication effects. Then it takes someone with econometric modeling skills to develop the model.

Even brands that invest heavily in data and talent still struggle to predict the future based on the past. Brands can develop models that demonstrate how communication has impacted the brand in the past. Past performance does not always guarantee the future.

Strategically, this is where you want to be. Just understanding the true impact of communication on sales is a very powerful tool. While the past may not totally predict the future, understanding the past offers a good framework on how to budget for the future.

Continual Testing

Test your way to success. One budgeting method is to continually be testing various budget scenarios in the marketplace. Perhaps you have an overall budget of $10 million. You construct a test market plan based on a $20 million budget level and another test where you spend no money on communication. Then you monitor the tests markets along with your base level $10 million plan to see what happens. What is the communication effect of doubling the budget? And what is the communication effect of spending no money at all?

By continually testing different spending levels, you should begin to get a handle on what budget level produces the best return for the brand. Unlike predictive or econometric modeling, this is marketplace testing. You are getting real results from the market.

Constructing marketplace tests are easy to do in theory. They can fall apart upon execution. Your goal is to find markets that are representative of the overall brand situation. That means that the consumer, competition and distribution dynamics all need to align to the average. That is not always the easiest thing to do, particularly since you have no control over the competition.

The other downside to marketplace testing is that it takes time to read the results. This is not a short-term process. It may take a year to understand the impact of the test. In the meantime, you may be either under- or over-spending on communication.

Testing is a strategic ingredient that should be a part of any brand's communication process. Coupling testing with one of the other budgeting approaches provides the brand with a long-term foundation for developing strategically sound budgets.

Fixed vs. Variable Budget Items

Brand communication is viewed by senior management largely as a variable budget or expense item. This means that if a company needs to reduce expenses in a given quarter, brand communication may be on the chopping block.

With that said, let's discuss the difference between fixed and variable budget items. A fixed budget item is what it sounds like. It is fixed. Just like you may pay rent or hold a mortgage, a company has certain expenses that are ongoing. Office rent is typically one of those fixed costs. A variable cost is more flexible. It may be a cost or program that can be eliminated or one that can be delayed. For example, the company may delay buying new office furniture. It is an expense that is flexible. You don't have to have it right now.

Within the brand communication budget, there are arguably fixed expenses. Let's review each of the three broad budget categories for items that could be considered fixed.

- In the Working Budget category, owned media should be considered a fixed expense. You wouldn't want to pull the plug on the brand's website or social media. This is where consumers engage with your brand. The brand may have entered into a long-term sponsorship or event contract that makes it de facto, fixed.

- In the Nonworking Budget category, research may be contracted for that renders it a relatively fixed cost. Could it be moved? Possibly. But, it may cost more to move it than to keep it where it is.
- In the Overhead and Fees Budget category, there are a number of items that while not totally fixed, are not extremely flexible. Those include agency contracts, software and subscription contracts, and brand employees. All of these can be eliminated but at a significant cost. With any personnel decision, you need to weigh the possible negative outcome such as loss of productivity and the human toll that it can take on someone's life.

The largest aspect of the communication budget that offers senior management a budget reduction opportunity is the paid media budget. Media purchases can be cancelled with proper notification. This can free up sometimes millions of dollars for a company to put to their bottom line. Paid media as well as production can also be delayed or pushed into another fiscal quarter if the company needs those dollars to meet a quarterly profit target.

Budget reductions are never fun. You hope that the senior management of the company views brand communication as an investment in growing the brand rather than an expense that can be easily cut. The reality is that budget reductions are a part of managing a company. As a brand communicator, you need to be aware that this is a possibility and plan accordingly.

Communication Budget Financial Implications

You don't need a degree in finance to develop a communication budget. However, you should be aware of how the communication budget is viewed from a financial perspective.

Brand communication is a part of the Selling, General and Administrative (SG&A) line item on a company's income statement. SG&A covers all expenses used by the company to promote, sell, and deliver the company's products to market. SG&A also includes all expenses that are a part of managing the company. So, brand communication is one aspect of SG&A.

If the brand you are working on is a publicly traded company or part of a publicly traded company, SG&A is a line item that security analysts use to judge the costs of sales. In essence, SG&A becomes an efficiency measure for the company. As a result, the brand's communication budget is under financial scrutiny. Security analysts compare the company's SG&A to their industry peer group as a guide to how efficiently the company generates revenue.

Knowing that this is the case is important as you develop your budgeting strategy. Brand communication is treated as an expense on the income statement. While we may feel that brand communication is an investment, the reality is that those financial analysts who impact a company's overall stock market capitalization view it differently. Even the value of a brand is viewed as an intangible rather than tangible asset on a company's balance sheet.

That doesn't mean that security analysts or those who may follow a company's financial performance do not think that brand communication has any value. They certainly do. What is important to note is that ultimately the CEO or CFO of the company must defend SG&A spending if it is significantly different than its industry peer group. You will need to make sure that the brand communication budget strategy clearly provides value for the brand and the company.

Summary

In summary, budgeting is a crucial strategic element in developing the brand communication program. The budget itself can be complex including paid media, owned media, and nonworking media line items. Depending upon the brand communication internal department and external resources, there is another layer of overhead costs and fees.

Developing a budget can be as complex as the budget itself. There are a number of strategic approaches. Each has its pros and cons. Budgeting can be internally focused using such methods as a percent of sales or all you can afford. Budgeting can be externally focused by benchmarking the brand's spending to the competition. One method is to spend at parity with other brands. Another method is called share of spending where your spending is set as a percent of the total spending in the category. Budgeting can be communication-based using methods such as objective/task or computer algorithm simulations. Budgeting can be marketplace-driven. This requires the brand to develop marketplace tests at various budget levels in order to determine the most effective spending level.

There is no right or wrong method to developing the budget. It largely depends upon the brand and company plus the level of data available to make the budget decision.

Regardless of the method, it is important to recognize that the brand communication budget is one of many brand and/or corporate budget items. From a financial perspective, the brand communication budget is largely a variable budget. This means that if the corporation needs to make budget reductions, the brand communication budget is vulnerable.

From an income statement perspective, the brand communication budget is a part of the Selling, General, and Administrative budget line item. This SG&A budget is one of many factors scrutinized by financial analysts when assessing the stock market value of the company.

Having a strategic point of view about budgeting is paramount in both developing as well as retaining the brand communication program.

Review Questions

1. What are the typical components of a communication budget?
2. What are the strategic approaches used in developing a communications budget? What are their strengths and weaknesses?
3. What is the difference between a fixed and variable budget item?
4. How is communication applied to a company's balance sheet? What is SG&A? How do security analysts use it?

Discussion Questions

1. What items should be included in a brand communication budget? How should this budget be viewed in terms of the marketing budget?
2. What is the best way to approach brand communication budgeting? Does it differ by the type of industry?

3. Go to the Investor Relations tab on the Coca-Cola website. In their annual report, find the SG&A number and percentage. Now go to PepsiCo and do the same thing. What are the similarities or differences?

Additional Resources

Kelley, L., D. Jugenheimer, and K. Sheehan. 2015. *Advertising Media Planning: A Brand Management Approach*. 4th ed. New York: Routledge.

Kotler, P. and G. Armstrong. 2013. *Principles of Marketing*. 15th ed. New York: Prentice-Hall.

Moriarty, S, N. Mitchell and W. Wells. 2015. *Advertising & IMC: Principles and Practices*. 10th ed. New York: Pearson.

Chapter 5

Competitive Insight: Foundation of Strategy

Learning Objectives

This chapter is intended to help you:

- Understand the components of competitive analyses
- Understand how to analyze the category dynamics
- Understand how to analyze competitive positioning and messaging
- Understand how to analyze competitive communication mix
- Understand how to analyze consumer and technology trends
- Learn to apply the analyses to strategic decision matrix

Components of Competitive Analyses

To know how to win, you need to understand the game, yourself, and your opponent(s). Only by understanding all three will you be able to craft a winning strategy whether it is on the field of battle, play, or in the marketplace.

As a brand communication professional, it is no different. In this chapter, we will discuss how to strategically evaluate the competitive landscape so that you can make the best strategic communication decisions for your brand.

There are four broad areas to evaluate:

1) **Category Dynamics**: An overview of the category that your brand is doing business in and how your brand compares to others in that marketplace.
2) **Competitive Positioning and Messaging:** How the competition is positioning their brands and how they are messaging to support their position.

3) **Competitive Communication Mix:** How the competition is allocating its communication dollars.
4) **Consumer Trends:** Consumer opportunities or threats that can impact the brand and its communication plans.

By analyzing each of these four areas, you can develop a strategic decision matrix that can help you determine the best opportunity for the brand. It is the interplay of the analysis that can help shape a winning strategy. The place to start is by analyzing the category. When evaluating the best opportunity for brand communication, you should consider answering the following three questions:

1) What is winning in this category?
2) Where will you play in the category?
3) How will you win?

Category Dynamics

Every category has its own dynamics and historical way of doing business. It is your job to review the category to understand how your brand will ultimately win. To do that, you need to understand the dynamics of the category itself and the competitors that make it up.

The first step is to understand the overall category. The following are a few key dimensions that should be summed up on a single page.

- How big is the category? This can mean total sales and/or number of customers.
- Is this category growing or shrinking?
- How does this category do business?

The key facts about any business category are the total revenue and its trajectory. If you are in a huge category with billions of dollars in revenue such as the automotive industry or a niche market such as dental floss, that will suggest different strategies.

For any category, it is important to understand if it is growing or shrinking. For example, the nonalcoholic liquid beverage refreshment industry is slightly growing yet soft drinks are declining while tea is growing. If you are marketing soft drinks, in order for your brand to grow, you need to take business from another brand. Conversely, if you are in the tea category, you may have a tailwind behind your growth aspirations.

Every category has a pattern of doing business a certain way. Sometimes brand communication can highlight that and provide an alternative. Ally Bank is an example of a brand that highlighted how banks typically do business and positioned themselves as the solution. Figure 5.1 is an example of an Ally Bank ad that takes on bank fees.

Figure 5.1
Ally Bank Ad for Checking

The other aspect of how a category does business is to understand the overall marketing mix and what really drives the category. The broad view of the marketing mix is summed up by the age-old 4Ps of marketing: Product, Price, Place (Distribution), and Promotion (i.e., Communication).

In a very competitive category such as fast food or quick service restaurants, you will find that the category is driven by new products and short-term promotions. This is an extremely competitive communication category with McDonald's, Burger King, Sonic, Carl's Jr., Hardee's, and many more competing for share of stomach. They all conform largely to the same formula of new product innovation and short-term promotion as their method for doing business. In this category, communication is vital.

On the other hand, let's look at an equally as competitive category—retail gasoline. This is a category driven largely by distribution so the fight is for real estate and not necessarily state of mind. In this category, communication is a distant cousin to distribution. The brand is promoted by who has the most convenient locations.

It is crucial to understand how a category does business and the role that communication plays in the business model. It can offer potential opportunities to break out of the mold of well-entrenched business practices. How your business does within this category may be driven by someone other than the brand manager. A CEO or a group of senior leadership professionals may dictate the overall business approach. So, a brand manager and the brand communication professionals may be put in a position to develop the most compelling communication within the context of the same business model as the overall category. This suggests that you must focus on using communication to help differentiate your brand since many of the other business methods for differentiation may be the same.

Once you understand the category, then you need to dive into the competition. Here is a checklist for the competition.

- How are the brands positioned?
- How do the brands message?
- How do they allocate their communication resources?

We will discuss each of these aspects of the competition in great detail in this chapter beginning with competitive positioning and messaging.

Competitive Positioning and Messaging

The foundation of brand messaging and communication is brand positioning. The majority of consumer categories have three classic marketplace positions: the most popular brand, the highest quality brand, and the least expensive brand. There are wide variations on these three themes. From a starting point in your evaluation process, you can begin to categorize brands into those three positions.

Let's take a look at the highly competitive auto insurance category as an example for these three categories.

- Most Popular: State Farm
- Highest Quality: Allstate
- Price Leader: Geico

These three brands have long been positioned in these categories. While there are many other companies that challenge these brands, these three are the leaders in each of these marketplace positions.

As you analyze each brand, one of the key components for brand positioning is the underlying reasons to believe (RTBs). RTBs are the rationale for why Geico can claim to provide the lowest price or why State Farm is the most popular brand. A compelling rationale leads to a compelling position.

When reviewing the brand positioning and reasons to believe, you should check the strength of the position. You can use the following three criteria:

1) Is it distinctive? (Can any other brand claim this same territory? Are the reasons to believe strong enough to build a moat around this position?)
2) Is it deliverable? (Is the brand actually delivering on the promise? If the brand is the price leader, does it actually have the lowest prices?)
3) Is it durable? (Brands should be positioned for the long haul. Is this a position that can be sustained?)

The auto insurance brands we highlighted have very compelling positions in the market with strong reasons to believe. The following is a brief recap of each brand:

- State Farm: Most Popular
  Reasons to Believe: State Farm is the leading auto insurer in the United States with nearly three times the customers and agents than the next leading auto insurer.
- Allstate: Highest Quality
  Reasons to Believe: Allstate provides the most comprehensive auto insurance covering damage ranging from natural disasters to animals to theft as well as collision.
- Geico: Price Leader
  Reasons to Believe: Geico does its business online without an agent model thereby reducing the overhead applied to insurance costs.

Each of these brands offers strong reasons to believe their position in the marketplace. While they are strong, there are competitors that certainly are challenging each of them and the positions that they occupy.

That means that how you say it is as important as what you say.

Once you have analyzed the competitive positions of each brand in the market, you next can analyze how they communicate their position.

Figure 5.2 shows a brand communication audit featuring the three auto insurance companies. The key dimensions for the communication audit are:

Figure 5.2
Communication Audit
Insurance Industry Example

Audit	State Farm	Allstate	Geico
Campaign Idea	Agents will take care of you no matter what	Don't buy cut rate insurance. Allstate is worth the money	Save 15% in 15 minutes
Tagline	Like a Good Neighbor, State Farm is there	You are in good hands	15 minutes saves 15%
Brand Dimensions	Variety of brand characters	Mayhem character Actor – Dennis Haysbert	Variety of brand characters

- What is the campaign idea?
- What is the tagline?
- What are key brand dimensions?

The campaign idea is the core idea of the communication. For example, State Farm's brand position of being the market leader is paid off with the campaign idea that State Farm agents will take care of you no matter what the circumstances. They way they do it is through a series of humorous vignettes that dramatize this idea. Their tagline, "Like a good neighbor, State Farm is there" is a brand positioning line.

Allstate's core idea is that if you buy less expensive insurance, you will be sorry. One way Allstate demonstrates this idea is through a character called "Mayhem" who wreaks havoc on unsuspecting people who are not covered by Allstate. Allstate's tagline is a branding line, "You're in good hands with Allstate."

Geico's core idea is that you can save 15 percent in 15 minutes by switching to Geico. Save 15 percent in 15 minutes is Geico's tagline as well as brand promise. Geico was one of the first auto insurance companies to effectively use brand characters and humor in their advertising. Over the years, Geico has introduced a wide variety of characters, situations, and metaphors that have been funny and engaging.

As you review the communication audit of these three brands, there are some very clear conclusions you can draw about this category. One is that these brands are very well positioned with strong campaign ideas that clearly pay off their marketplace positions. The second is that they now all use some form of humor in their advertising. And third, they all use some form of brand character(s).

Based on the brand positioning and communication audit, you can begin to develop a frame of reference for how your brand should communicate. Coupling what the category is saying with how much and where they are spending provides a complete communication view of the category.

Competitive Communication Mix

Understanding where and how much your competitors are investing in various media provides insight into how you can best allocate your resources. For example, if the category only spends their advertising dollars in television, you have plenty of other media alternatives for your message to stand out.

The first step in the process is to do an audit of your competition. Chart out what communication channels they use, how much they spend by channel and, when they spend it. Fortunately, there are secondary resources such as Kantar Media's Competitive Media Reports or CMR that provide this type of information. Kantar is the industry leader. There are others in this space. As you utilize competitive information, make sure that you include the entire communication spectrum of paid media. This includes not only broadcast, print, digital, and out-of-home media but sponsorships, events, and social media. Try to get as detailed as possible.

Once you have created a grid, you can then begin to see patterns emerge. You will find that many brands use a similar communication mix with the only difference being how much they allocate to each communication channel. This is largely driven by the perceived need to not let the competition "own" a certain media channel and that the target audience for that category has similar media habits. Using the same communication mix goes back to the idea that most categories do business a certain way. Allocating communication resources can fall into that trap.

Now that you have information about how your competitors allocate their communication dollars, you can take it one step further and develop a communication strategic matrix. Figure 5.3 represents this approach. The two axes for the strategic matrix are competitive clutter and target media usage composition. The first axis, competitive clutter, comes from the competitive media analysis. Media categories and media vehicles that are used by the majority of the category fall on the right side of the grid. Those media categories or vehicles that are used sparingly fall on the left side of the grid. You can visually get a good handle on where the category is allocating its resources.

The second axis adds the consumer's media habits into the equation. Have your media team utilize secondary resources such as Media Mark Research (MRI) or Simmons Market Research Bureau (SMRB) to determine the media categories and vehicles that offer the strongest composition of your target market. The media vehicles that are strong fall above the line. Those that are weak, fall below the line.

As you review Figure 5.3, you will see which communication vehicles are the most highly used by the target market. You will also see those communication vehicles which are not only highly used by the

Figure 5.3
Competitive Communication
Strategic Analysis

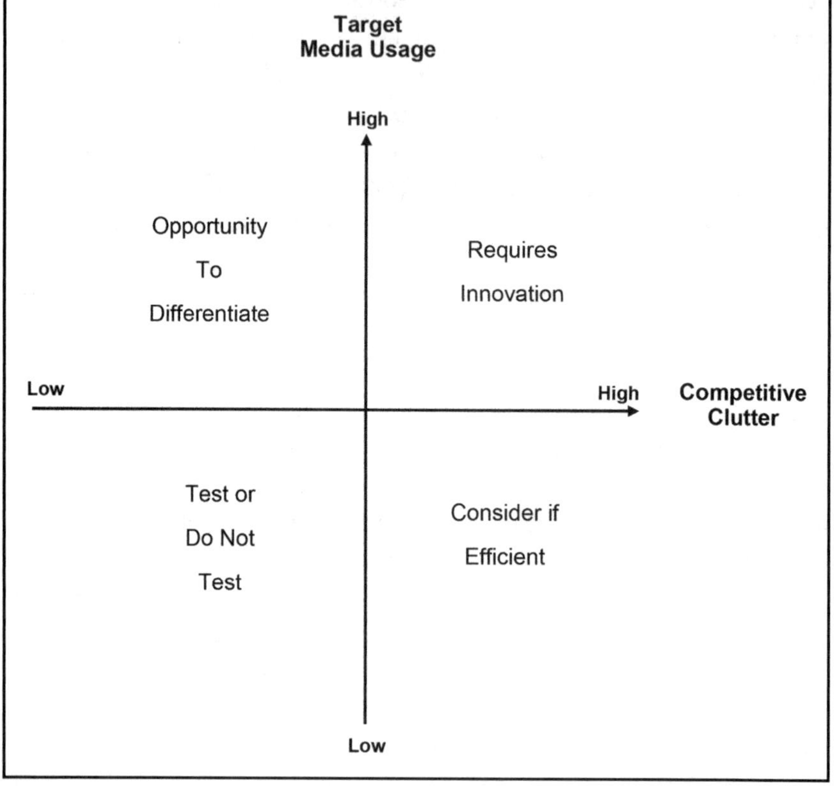

target market and not widely used by the competition. The communication vehicles in this group offer the greatest opportunity for competitive differentiation. Those are the vehicles you may elect to allocate some resources to before the competition gets aggressive. The top right corner of the matrix consists of vehicles that are important to your target yet have a strong competitive presence. In this case, you must be innovative to stand out in a cluttered environment. The bottom of the matrix contains the vehicles that are less popular with the target. For that reason, the left side of the quadrant consists of vehicles that are not used by the competition. The right side contains vehicles that may reach your target but are less targeted than others. For example, the Super Bowl may reach your target but it also reaches many consumers who are not in your target. For this quadrant, you need to be selective before committing your resources.

Figure 5.4 contains a bare-bones example of how to use this strategic analysis. This example is for the domestic beer category based on broadcast programming types using frequent beer drinkers as the target market.

It is no surprise that sports programming appeals to this audience and that it is a very competitive arena. Most of the major domestic beer brands have a presence in sports programming. Those same beer brands also have a strong presence in top-rated network television programming.

Figure 5.4
Beer Category Example

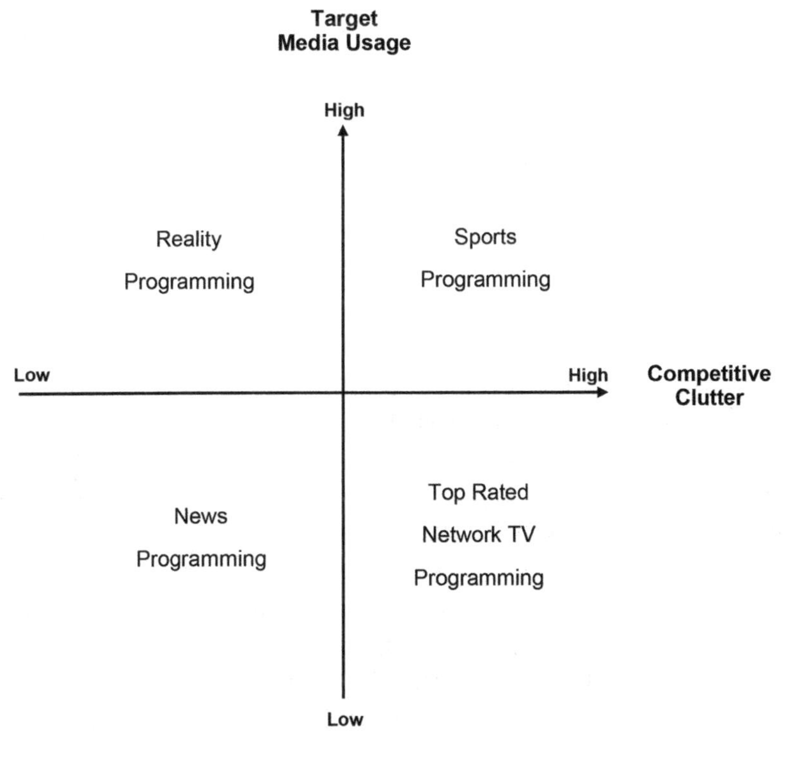

While this programming may not be as targeted as sports, it offers significant reach potential which appeals to this category. On the other side, reality and news programming have a relatively weak presence in terms of category communication. News programming skews older consumers compared to the young beer drinking consumer so it is not an appealing area. However, reality programming could be a true area of opportunity.

This approach to categorizing communication mix opportunities is not limited to television programming. At a macro-level, it can be used to assess overall communication mix opportunities. At a micro-level, it can provide a tactic, such as the reality programming in the beer category, that can offer the brand an opportunity for differentiation.

Consumer and Technology Trends

Consumer trends are not usually associated with competitive analysis. Yet, they provide some of the richest areas of strategic opportunity for any brand. There are three broad categories of trends that should be considered from a competitive perspective. They are:

1) Consumer demographics
2) Consumer behavior and attitudes
3) Technology innovation

The first trend to consider as a part of your competitive analysis is consumer demographic trends. The one aspect of consumer demographic trends is that you can incorporate them into your strategic thinking on a long-term basis since they evolve over time.

As you review consumer demographic trends for your brand, you should do so in three ways. The first is to understand how consumer trends may impact who is buying your brand. The second is to understand the competitive strengths or weaknesses of these trends within the category. The third is to understand how the category is adjusting its communication to account for these trends.

For example, if you are working on a diaper brand in the United States, it should be clear that the ethnic composition of mothers and their babies is changing. Over the past 20 years, the percentage of Hispanic children has nearly tripled. As of 2015, the percentage of non-Caucasian children being born is exceeding that of Caucasian children. This trend suggests that your brand needs to develop communication that addresses an ethnically diverse group of mothers.

Knowing that you need to be mindful to address a growing ethnically diverse population, you should analyze how the category, the competition, and your brand are attracting this new audience. Is your brand attracting these groups at a higher rate than the category? Is the category attracting these new audiences? What are the competitive opportunities to attract and retain these growing market segments? A thorough competitive analysis of market demographics of the category and competitive brands will be valuable to help guide your future communication decisions.

The third aspect to understanding consumer trends is how the category and competitive brands are addressing these changes. For example, are competitive brands investing paid media dollars to address these emerging segments? Are there communication channels and/or messages for these new audiences that have yet to be addressed? By identifying these trends, you may be able to gain the "first mover" advantage in a growth market.

The second consumer trend that goes hand-in-glove with demographics is consumer behavior and attitudes. Just like demographic trends, consumer behavior and attitudinal trends have longitudinal measures that provide great guidance to future forecasting.

For example, based on the ongoing Gallup poll of consumer attitudes in the United States, the percent of the population that believes that three-plus children is the ideal number to have has dropped from 66 percent in 1936 to 32 percent in 1980. By 2014, that number now had dropped into the mid-20s. If you are marketing diapers, it is important to know that the prevailing sentiment is to have fewer than three children per household.

Another trend that could impact the diaper market is the growing environmental movement. There is a growing consumer attitude that diapers and other items that are not biodegradable have a negative environmental impact. There is a long list of articles citing the environmental hazards of the disposable diaper. Acknowledging or participating in this conversation could give a diaper brand a possible point of differentiation.

The third trend is technology innovations that can impact communication. Over the past 20 years, there have been a number of technological disruptions in the communication industry. The Internet, smartphones, and social media are three big technological innovations that are changing the way we communicate.

Just about every day, it seems that there is a new social media app designed for smartphone use that is replacing an existing one. While you may not want to chase every new social media platform, you may find some emerging communication channel that offers your brand a leg up in the marketplace.

For example, if you are using pictures and video to help tell your brand's story, then social media photo sharing apps such as Instagram or Snapchat may become appealing. Or video apps such as Meerkat may provide a unique venue. Perhaps you want to build a brand experience. New virtual reality content from Facebook's Oculus Rift and others may offer your brand a new way to gain consumer engagement. The list of new technologies goes on and on. The point is that you should analyze these technologies from a similar vein as the existing communication mix channels. Are there new channels that have a strong potential for your target market? And can you be the first to stake out a significant position within that channel?

In today's rapid-fire world, embracing technology change for your brand's communication is vital to its long-term success. By closely following media technology trends, you have the opportunity to put your brand ahead of others in your category's communication space.

Strategic Matrix (SWOT)

Now it is time to put all of this competitive knowledge together. We have used a strategic matrix to analyze the communication mix. We can take that same approach to analyze the entire communication strategy. Figure 5.5 is a strategic matrix that follows the SWOT analysis. SWOT stands for strengths, weaknesses, opportunities, and threats. In this matrix, we will apply the SWOT thinking to brand communication and any factor that impacts it.

Strengths and weaknesses are areas that can be impacted now. These are items that are either strong or weak today. Opportunities and threats are areas that can help or hinder the brand in the future. Together, this matrix allows you to develop what-if scenarios for the brand and its communication.

Brand strengths are something that you are doing better than the competition. For example, your brand's social media presence is the category

Figure 5.5
Competitive Strategy Matrix
Today vs. Tomorrow

	Strengths	**Weaknesses**
Today	Build on Core Strengths	Barriers to Taking Advantage
Tomorrow	Poised to Take Advantage	Survivability Is Threatened
	Opportunities	**Threats**

leader. A brand weakness on the other hand may be the lack of resources compared to the category. Your brand is underfunded in the area of communication.

Opportunities are those trends that you have analyzed. For example, social media is gaining ground as an important communication platform. Threats can be increased spending by the competition. Or if network television is an important medium to your communication mix, then the erosion of its audience could pose a threat.

As you plot these items into their respective quadrants, you will find that it will begin to help paint a picture of what steps to take to maximize your strategy. For example, if your brand is strong in social media and your know that social media is growing, then you may want to make an investment in a team of social media specialists dedicated to working this channel. Hiring a social media team is an inexpensive way to gain a media presence compared to spending dollars on paid media. So, if your budget is less than the other brands in the category, then this strategy looks to be a winner.

By working the strategic matrix, you can begin to find areas of opportunity for your brand's communication. To make the matrix most effective, you may want to approach its use by asking various strategic questions. For example, what are the best communication vehicles that would offer the brand a competitive advantage in the market? Use the matrix to identify vehicles where you are strong or weak; the matrix can also recognize growth opportunities and audience erosion. Or you can ask a question about what are the key brand dimensions to consider. This could elicit an idea about using music or developing a brand character. The strategic matrix is very flexible and can be used however best fits

Summary

In summary, there are four key competitive areas to analyze when developing your brand communication strategy. The first area is category dynamics. This is the fundamentals of the category. Included are key market drivers such as product innovation, differentiation, price, distribution, and overall promotion. This is the first step to determine the strengths and weaknesses of your brand. The second area is brand positioning and messaging. This area provides context on how the competition is positioned in the market, how strong that position is, and how each brand expresses that position. From this analysis, you will have the context for developing future communication. The third area is the communication mix. This is where the category is placing its communication. This analysis includes paid, earned, and owned media. From this analysis, you will gain context on how best to allocate your resources. The fourth area is key trends that impact the brand's communication. These include consumer demographic trends, consumer attitudes and behavior, plus technology innovations that impact future communication. These trends provide context for developing areas of opportunities and/or threats to your future strategies.

By using a strategic matrix, you can bring all of these elements together. The strategic matrix provides a method to quickly analyze strengths, weaknesses, opportunities, and threats for the brand and its communication program. This analysis sets the stage for developing insights that can lead to future strategic recommendations.

Review Questions

1. What are the components of a competitive analysis?
2. What is the difference between brand positioning and messaging?
3. What is the competitive communication matrix? How do you use it to identify opportunities?
4. What three consumer trends should be analyzed to provide context to the competitive framework?
5. What is the strategic matrix? How would you use it to make a decision?

Discussion Questions

1. Can you think of any other competitive aspects that would influence how you ultimately crafted a communication strategy?
2. Review the running shoe category. How are the key brands positioned? What are their main messages? Is there clear differentiation in the category?
3. What are the most compelling consumer demographic and attitudinal trends that are facing the food industry?
4. What communication technology do you think will be the next big disruptor in the marketplace?

Additional Resources

Kelley, L. and D. Jugenheimer. 2015. *Advertising Account Planning: Planning and Managing an IMC Campaign* 3rd ed. New York: Routledge.

Kelley, L., D. Jugenheimer, and K. Sheehan. 2015. *Advertising Media Planning: A Brand Management Approach*. 4th ed. New York: Routledge.

Porter, M. 1998. *Competitive Strategy: Techniques for Analyzing Industries and Competitors*. New York: Free Press.

Rumelt, R. P. 2011. *Good Strategy Bad Strategy: The Difference and Why It Matters*. New York: Random House.

Chapter 6

Target Market Strategy

Learning Objectives

This chapter is intended to help you:

- Understand the methods for segmenting the target market
- Understand how to apply target segmentation to the brand purchase funnel
- Understand the interplay of purchaser/user/influencer
- Understand segmentation vs. aggregation
- Understand the interaction of all stakeholders in developing a target
- Understand strategic alternatives in targeting

Introduction

Who to target is one of the most important strategic decisions a brand can make. After all, who you target is destined to dictate your approach to communication. Understanding why you are targeting this consumer group helps you define the consumer motivation.

While targeting is so crucial to the success of the brand from both marketing and a brand communication perspective, it is sometimes baffling why there isn't more strategic thought put into the process. Many brands pick up last year's plan and target the same audience year after year. These are the brands that wonder why they can't grow their customer base.

Understanding who the brand's consumers are, how frequently they purchase your brand, and what motivates them to make that purchase provides a framework for strategically segmenting your target market.

Developing a target market strategy requires looking at the business opportunity and the ability to use communication as a strategic asset to mine that opportunity.

From a business perspective, it is simple. Every brand wants to grow. The question is how to do it? From a behavioral standpoint, there are just a few paths to success. One is to add new users to the brand. The other is to get current users to use the brand more often. Or there is a combination of the two.

There are a number of ways to add new users to the brand:

- Switch users within the category to your brand;
- Return lapsed users to your brand; and
- Expand the category to attract new category and brand users.

Each of these paths dictates how you might communicate. If you are trying to persuade a Ford owner to switch to a Chevy, that will require finding a compelling reason to switch. On the other hand, if you are trying to gain the return of lapsed users, this requires communicating a totally different message. And convincing someone to substitute a SUV for a truck may be a different communication strategy yet.

The decision on how best to grow the brand has a marked impact on how to target the message. These decisions lead to how to best segment the target audience to gain the most leverage on strategically growing the brand with the resources available.

Segmentation Methods

Figure 6.1 is a graphic representation of the stages of segmentation. Each stage of the segmentation pyramid builds on the other. As you can see, as you move up the pyramid, the segmentation goes from reviewing facts and figures to diving deeper into emotional motivation. Let's review each stage and why you may consider using it to strategically define your target market.

The base level of segmentation defines who is buying the brand. It may seem rather obvious to know who is buying the brand. If you are selling oil field equipment, you may actually know the names of the people buying the brand. However, if you are selling a can of beans, you may have millions of buyers.

That is the point of the first stage of segmentation. You need to understand the framework of your target market. How many people are in your

Figure 6.1
Segmentation Pyramid

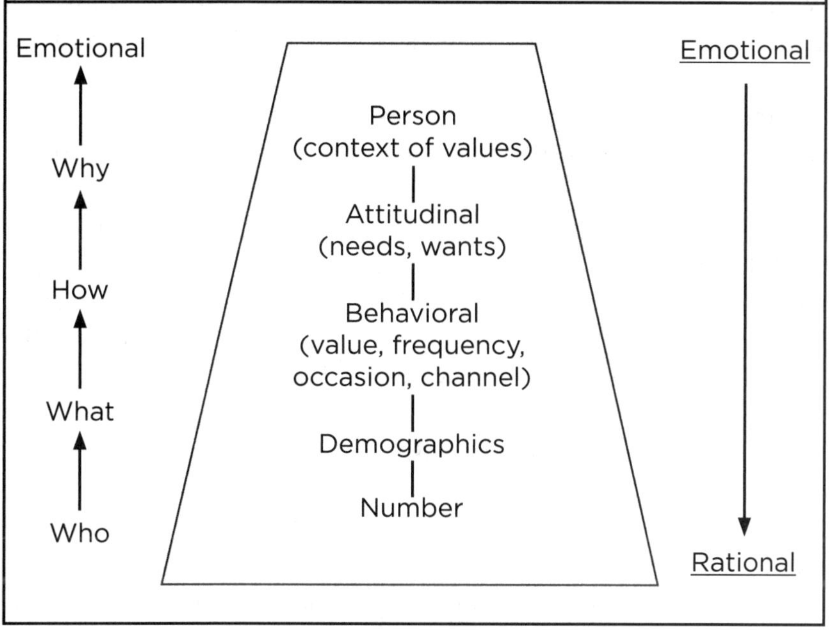

market? As we mentioned, if you are marketing oil field equipment then you may be able to count the number of customers on your hand. If you are marketing a can of beans, you may not be able to personally count the number of consumers buying your product. However, you may be able to personally count the number of grocery stores who agree to stock your item on their shelves. Fortunately, through point-of-sale software that most grocery stores use, you will be able to get a count of the number of consumers buying your brand plus the number of consumers buying any and all canned beans. Together, these numbers will tell you quite a bit about your standing in the canned bean market.

Understanding if these numbers are growing or shrinking indicates the vitality of the market and what role your brand plays in that marketplace.

These simple numbers add considerable context to your overall segmentation approach.

The second stage of the segmentation pyramid goes after the "what." What do you know about your customers? A good place to start is with demographics for consumer goods and job titles for business-to-business markets.

Strategically, you will want to understand the composition of the audience of your brand so you can compare it to other brands in the category. For example, suppose the majority of your brand's buyers are over the age of 50, yet the majority of the category buyers are under the age of 50. This may suggest that there is an opportunity for your brand to gain younger users. Or, it may suggest that your brand may not appeal to younger users. So, you may need to conduct research to understand why there is such an age disparity between your brand and the category.

Application to Purchase Funnel

Brands routinely analyze their consumer base to understand where there may be a barrier and/or opportunity to grow the brand. Many times this research is plotted in the form of a brand purchase funnel. Sometimes the purchase funnel is called the consumer pathway or customer journey.

Figure 6.2 provides a representation of a typical brand purchase funnel. The steps in the funnel correlate to steps in the consumer purchase process. In this case the five steps are:

1) Awareness: Becoming aware of the brand.
2) Consideration: Putting the brand in the considered purchase set.
3) Purchase: Buying the brand.
4) Repeat Purchase: Buying the brand more than one time.
5) Loyalty: Buying only that brand in the category.

When evaluating who to target, identifying the problem is the first step. For example, if the brand has over 90 percent awareness among consumers, targeting those who are unaware of the brand may not be an opportunity target. However, if the brand has only 20 percent awareness, this may signal that you should consider targeting those who are unaware of the brand.

Once consumers are aware of your brand, the next step in the purchase funnel process is to gain consideration. This means that if someone is in

Figure 6.2
Brand Purchase Funnel

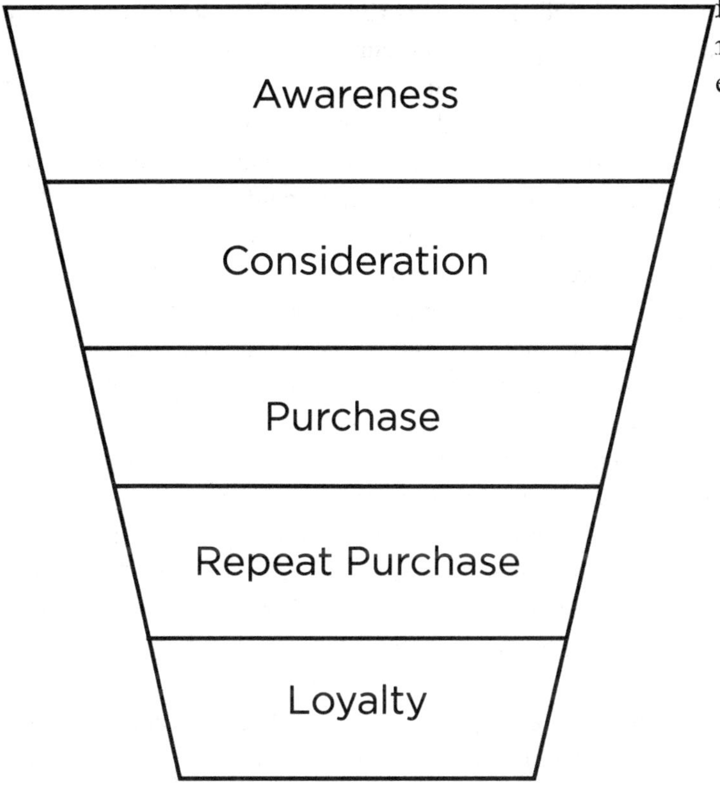

The next level of the purchase funnel is actually purchasing the brand. Obviously, this is a key metric and group. Like the other stages of the purchase funnel, you can target those who purchase the brand or those who don't. An important opportunity segment is the consumer who considers purchasing your brand yet doesn't. This means that you haven't convinced him/her to make that leap from thinking about it to doing it. If you can crack the code with this group, you have a direct path to gaining more brand purchases.

Another important group is the repeat purchase consumer. Like the previous stages of the purchase funnel, getting someone who has already purchased the brand to continue to buy it is a strong way to maintain brand revenue. In this stage of the purchase funnel, it is important to develop dimensions of purchase frequency. Once they have purchased the brand, you may elect to understand those who bought it once yet didn't buy it again. Then you may segment the other brand purchasers into groups based on how frequently they buy the brand. For example, a light user may be someone who buys it once or twice while a medium user may be purchasing it three to six times and a heavy user may be purchasing it six or more times. Every brand will have some form of consumer purchase frequency; for instance, a consumer packaged good like ketchup may be purchased once a month while an automobile may be purchased once every five years. For those brands with a short purchase cycle such as a consumer package good (ketchup), targeting by frequency of usage is an important method for segmenting the target.

The final stage of the purchase funnel is loyalty. Loyalty in this case means that the consumer only buys your brand regardless of the competition. There is an industry built around rewarding loyal users in just about every consumer product category. Targeting loyal users is a strategy to maintain your user base. It may not be the most effective way to grow your user base since they may be at their limit of brand usage. It is important to note that it takes many users to make up for the loss of a loyal user. So, while targeting this group may be more of a defensive move, it certainly has merit.

Some brands look at one more stage of loyalty. That is brand advocacy. This is where a loyal user becomes an apostle for your brand. Loyal Apple users fall into this category. They are fiercely loyal to Apple. As a result, they are quick to tell others how great Apple is. When this group takes to social media, the brand can generate some terrific word-of-mouth advertising. Encouraging loyal users to not only stay true to the brand but to tell others about it is an important target opportunity.

Developing a segmentation strategy based on brand purchase dynamics is a valuable method to approach targeting. This is particularly true when the brand can isolate the specific stages in the purchase funnel that may be blocked. Not only does this provide a solid underpinning to the target strategy, it offers the opportunity to measure future success.

Interplay of Purchaser/User/Influencer

It does seem rather obvious that you need to know as much as you can about who is buying your brand. However, just because the person is the purchaser, doesn't necessarily mean they are the most important target. The purchaser in many cases is not the user of the product. For example, mom may be the purchaser for all sorts of grocery items. Her list may be influenced by the user whether it is her children or a spouse. Since mothers make over 80 percent of the purchases for a household, they make the ultimate purchase decision. However, if you only target her, you could miss an opportunity to control what she purchases.

Another person in the purchasing dynamic is the influencer. This is a person who is not the purchaser or the user of the product. However, this person may have greater influence over the actual purchase decision than either the purchaser or user. This is particularly true in consumer products where there is technical expertise. For example, the purchaser may rely on a pharmacist's advice before purchasing an over-the-counter medicine for their sick child or spouse. Or a young adult may consult their parents about purchasing a car.

The purchase influence dynamic is very much in play in business decisions. If a company is buying software, the department head may be the user, the finance department may be the purchaser, and the IT department may be the influencer. And within the department, those who will ultimately use the software may also be important influencers. In this case, it is important to cover all your bases when making this type of sale.

Segmentation vs. Aggregation

We have discussed a lot about finding the best target audience segment to grow the brand. As you can see, there are a lot of ways to approach segmentation. Because you rarely have the resources to target an entire marketplace, segmentation finds the differences in that market that makes targeting more accessible.

Segmentation is about finding market differences. Aggregation, on the other hand, is about finding commonalities. When you approach the target from a marketing perspective, segmentation is crucial. When you approach the market from a brand message perspective, aggregation is crucial.

Aggregation is where you find common consumer values that can form the foundation for your message strategy. You build an overall message platform that can cut across various target segments. Then you tailor the specific message to the nuances of each segment.

For example, Coke's overall theme is built on the idea that having a Coke will make you happy. That is the overall theme or idea. Happiness can be very different for different people. So, the way you translate the message of happiness may be different for a mom versus a teenage boy. While the specific messages are different, the underlying idea is the same.

As you go through the segmentation process, it is important to constantly find common ground among the market segments. This will provide the brand with a strong message platform that will resonate with each segment plus will reinforce the bigger idea.

All Brand Stakeholders

When you are working to grow a consumer brand, you focus on understanding the consumer. It is the obvious thing to do. If you pull back from the consumer purchase interaction with the brand, you will find that there are a variety of other stakeholders who are extremely important to the brand's short- and long-term success. There are both inside and outside forces that should be taken into consideration.

Let's look first at stakeholders within the brand's organization. There are the associates who actually work on the brand itself, senior management, and the investment community. All of these stakeholders can impact the brand.

Sometimes the most powerful brand allies are your own employees. That is especially true of a service brand. If you are a retailer, restaurant, or any other service brand, how your employees ultimately perform is vital to the outcome. Knowing this, you may elect to target your employees with a message or develop an incentive contest based on your campaign. These tactical actions may be as important as the consumer campaign itself.

How management and company investors view your brand can have a big impact on its future funding. If management shares your passion for the brand, then you may find that the company approval process becomes streamlined. If the investor community is excited about the brand, then a campaign can lead to increased investment in the company that ultimately can impact funding for your brand. For a publicly traded company, a small rise in the stock price can sometimes mean millions of additional dollars in market capitalization. A brand communication program could more than pay for itself with a small stock price move.

Externally, there are important stakeholders. The biggest is the brand's customers. For example, if you are working on a consumer packaged goods brand, then your customer is likely to be a grocery chain such as Kroger or a big box chain such as Walmart. You may sell to convenience stores, drugstores, or institutions such as schools or the military. Gaining and keeping distribution is job one for your brand. If your brand isn't on the shelf, no one can buy it.

There should be a strategic discussion about the role that brand communication may play with the brand's customers. This is particularly true in the consumer goods arena. Retailers can wield considerable power. It is worth the time to discuss if the customer should be considered as a target segment. For example, a relatively small regional sausage brand targeted their advertising solely at the category buyer for each grocery chain by placing billboards along the route that they drove from home to work. Then they found out what radio station each buyer listened to and purchased ads during commuting hours. The end result was a campaign that looked bigger than life to each buyer. It leads to more shelf space and ultimately more brand sales.

In other cases, a brand campaign could contain a promotional component that may include winning a trip or tickets to a sporting event. All of these "perks" can add up when the brand is courting customers who are the bridge to the brand's consumers.

The media is an important consideration in any brand campaign. In today's digital media environment, the media can be anyone from a national media platform to an influencer who has a popular blog or video presence. Cultivating these potential brand influencers can lead to increased earned media support that can help elevate the brand's campaign.

Another outside audience that is sometimes overlooked is friends, family, and potential employees. Friends and family can become important word-of-mouth advocates for the brand. Potential employees can be influenced by brand messages. Many human resource departments time their recruiting to brand campaigns knowing that it can lead to higher caliber candidates.

Strategic Alternatives

There are many ways to segment your brand's target market. It can be done through demographics, purchase behavior, or even psychological need state. All are viable and are commonly used in defining a target market. As we have discussed, a target market is not always the consumer. It can consist of a variety of stakeholders from customers to employees.

The strategic questions you need to ask yourself when developing a target market for your brand are:

- Where is the source of the most growth for the brand?
- What are your resource limitations to achieve growth?
- What is required to persuade that target market?

As you assess who is the best target market for the brand, it is important to understand the strategic levers of dollars and persuasion. The first is that amount of money at your disposal to actually develop a campaign. The second is what you need to say to convince someone to take the action you desire.

These latter two resources are crucial to understand if you can tackle the biggest source of growth for your brand. Let's discuss some examples.

- Imagine you are doing the brand communication for Dr Pepper. You may analyze the market and conclude that the biggest opportunity for growth is to convert loyal Coca-Cola users to Dr Pepper. After all, Coca-Cola has many more users than Dr Pepper. Now consider that Coca-Cola has considerably more monetary resources than Dr Pepper and even controls many of the bottling plants that produce Dr Pepper, you can see that this "master plan" has some large obstacles.
- Now imagine that you are Chevrolet. You want to convert Ford users to your brand. You may have the monetary resources to pull it off. But, can you find a message that is persuasive enough to do the trick? If you are attempting to do this in Michigan where both Ford and Chevrolet have significant

> manufacturing plants, you may be hard pressed to find a compelling argument to convert a die-hard Ford owner to switch allegiance to the "evil" Chevrolet brand.

Just as we have discussed in prior chapters, the goal is to help the brand find a competitive advantage in the marketplace that will propel its growth. This requires evaluating different target opportunities. Before just targeting brand users or category users, you must step back and truly assess the landscape of the marketplace. Is there a compelling target market that has been overlooked by the competition? This may be the quickest path to growth. Or is there a target opportunity that can propel your brand into the consumer's consciousness? For example, when Opray Winfrey purchased a stake in Weight Watchers, the brand saw tremendous growth based on her star power. Powerful brand influencers can sometimes elevate the brand more rapidly than a multimillion dollar advertising campaign.

As you develop a target market, have a session where you develop target market "what if" scenarios. What if we targeted Hispanics? What if we looked outside the category for growth? What if we got the endorsement of a key influencer? By developing scenarios and then filtering each one based on the questions of resources and persuasion ability, you can strategically develop a target market or series of target markets that can help the brand grow.

Summary

In summary, defining your target market is one of the most important strategic decisions for brand communication. The target market drives the message and media selection for the brand. It is crucial to understand how to best define the target to provide the brand with an opportunity to grow.

From a marketing standpoint, there are a limited number of ways to grow the brand. You can either add new users, get existing users to buy more often, switch competitive users to the brand, return lapsed users to the brand, or seek an entirely new audience. The marketing target will have a large impact on how the brand communication program unfolds.

There are a number of ways to segment a target market. Segmentation can be done demographically, behaviorally, or by need state. Another popular method of segmenting an audience is to understand the consumer behavior mapped to the brand purchase funnel. This involves the opportunity to segment a brand's audience based on awareness of the brand, purchase consideration of the brand, usage, and even loyalty or advocacy.

The dynamics of a brand's audience can be complex. There are purchasers of the brand, users of the brand, and possibly influencers. A brand purchaser may or may not necessarily be the ultimate user of the brand. This creates a segmentation opportunity. For some brands, there are influencers who can wield considerable power over the purchaser.

Once the target market is developed, there are message implications for brand communication. Approaching messaging requires the understanding of how each target segment is unique plus how they are similar. This is the difference between segmentation and aggregation. The goal of aggregation is to find a common message that unites the segments. Then segmentation offers the opportunity to tailor that overall message to each discreet group.

Not all target markets are consumer based. The brand has a variety of stakeholders to consider when developing a target. This can range from internal audiences to customers to investors.

In the final analysis, because defining the target is so important, it is in the best interest of the brand communication professional to develop a series of strategic alternatives. This exercise provides the opportunity to weigh the pros and cons of different target market approaches. This will lead to the development of a target market that provides a strategic advantage for the brand.

Review Questions

1. What are the key ways to target that will add new users to the brand?
2. What are the different stages of the segmentation pyramid? How might you use each to define a target market?
3. How can you map the target market to the brand's purchase funnel?
4. Can you describe the interplay between the user of a brand, its purchaser, and a possible purchase influencer?
5. How do you use the concept of segmentation and aggregation to construct a target market?

6. How should a brand review its target markets when considering all of its stakeholders?
7. What are the key questions that shape how you develop a target market that offers your brand a strategic opportunity?

Discussion Questions

1. Can you find examples of brands that have used targeting based on switching competitive users to their brand? How about targeting lapsed users? Or trying to expand the category to attract new category users?
2. Can you think of a time when it may be to the brand's advantage to target its current users?
3. What methods of communication do you feel are most appropriate for conveying the brand's message to internal brand stakeholders?
4. What is the difference between a marketing target and a brand communication target?

Additional Resources

Kelley, L. and D. Jugenheimer. 2015. *Advertising Account Planning: Planning and Managing an IMC Campaign*. 3rd ed. New York: Routledge.

Kelley, L, D. Jugenheimer and K. Sheehan. 2015. *Advertising Media Planning: A Brand Management Approach*. 4th ed. New York: Routledge.

Chapter 7

Place and Time Strategies

Learning Objectives

This chapter is intended to help you:

- Understand how to analyze geographic opportunities
- Understand how to analyze seasonality opportunities
- Understand the economics of geographic and seasonal advertising
- Understand strategic and tactical place and time approaches

Place and Time Answer Where and When

As we discussed in the previous chapter, nothing is more important to developing a strategic brand communication program than the target market. It forms the base of the brand's strategic foundation. The other two building blocks to this foundation are place and time.

Together, they form the basis for leveraging brand communication across the dimensions of who, where, and when. Each of these areas is critical to gaining a strategic advantage in the marketplace. The message strategy and execution answer the final questions of how and why.

Place is geography or where to communicate. This can be a market or a house or a physical location such as a grocery store. Where you elect to communicate has a huge impact on the brand's effectiveness.

Time is seasonality or timing of when to communicate. This can be a time of year, time of day, and the frequency and/or impact of that communication. Just like place, the timing of your message can have a big impact on the ultimate outcome of the brand communication program.

In this chapter, we are going to explore how you can analyze and use each of these two strategic levers to increase the effectiveness of your brand communication program. Let's first start by looking at how to analyze geographic opportunities.

Analyzing Geographic Opportunities

How you approach geographic support and messaging can offer tremendous strategic opportunities to grow the brand. The first step is to understand the brand's strengths and weaknesses relative to the category.

One way to analyze strengths and weaknesses is to review brand and category sales on a per capita basis. The classic method to construct this analysis is by developing a brand and category index for each geographic market. Commonly referred to as a BDI (Brand Development Index) and CDI (Category Development Index), each market index provides a quick snapshot of the relative sales strength of the brand and category.

Let's take a look at an example. Imagine you are marketing a picante sauce. About 3.4 percent of your brand's sales are concentrated in the Dallas/Ft. Worth, Texas area. The Dallas/Ft. Worth Nielsen Television market represents 1.7 percent of the U.S. population. The BDI for your picante sauce brand is 200 (3.4/1.7 × 100). So, Dallas is a good market for your brand.

Now, you want to see how strong your brand is compared to the category. Dallas/Ft. Worth represents 4.3 percent of the total category sales of picante sauce. This is a CDI of 300 (4.3/1.7 × 100).

When you review Figure 7.1, it shows that Dallas is represented in the "Star" quadrant. This is the quadrant where both the brand and category development are strong. These are markets that warrant support. Now take a look at San Antonio. It is in the quadrant labeled "Question Mark." San Antonio's brand development index is just 80 yet the category index for picante sauce is 400. This is a great picante sauce market yet your brand isn't doing that well. That is why this quadrant is named "Question Mark". On the surface, San Antonio should be a terrific market for your picante sauce brand yet it is underperforming. The question is "why?"

The answer to this question can dictate whether brand communication is the best solution to the problem. Among the problems that brand communication can solve are making consumers aware of the brand or changing the perception about the brand. Perhaps the problem in San Antonio is neither of these.

In this example, the answer to the brand's underperformance is that

Figure 7.1
Picante Sauce BDI/CDI Example

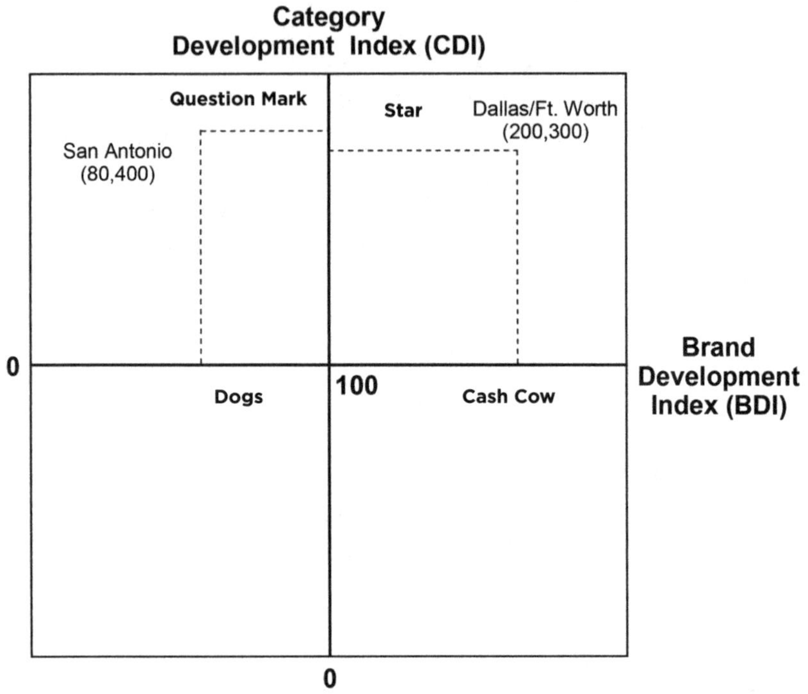

the largest grocery chain in San Antonio, HEB, is not carrying the brand. While consumers like your brand and may be familiar with it; they are restricted from buying it. Until the brand gains distribution at this key retail outlet, pouring broad market brand support may not be the solution to the problem. Gaining distribution should be the primary goal in this case. Once distribution is achieved, then brand communication can play a larger role in growing this market.

The other two quadrants in the geographic analysis chart are labeled "Dogs" and "Cash Cow." Dog markets contain weak brand and category development. In our picante sauce example, these are markets that don't like picante sauce in general nor your specific brand. It would take a lot of effort to convince consumers in these markets to buy your brand since you are working to convince them of the general category as well as your brand.

Cash Cow markets reflect where your brand is strong yet the category is relatively weak. The reference to "cash cow" refers to "milking the brand." This old-fashioned term means that you should collect the profit from these markets and use those funds to support growth markets. The challenge in a "cash cow" market is to grow the category. In these markets, it is not enough to convince consumers to like your brand; you must also find new ways for consumers to think about the entire category. Both Cash Cow and Dog markets are challenging from a brand communication perspective. Each may require considerable investment and perhaps a totally different brand communication approach.

The BDI/CDI analysis provides a strong analytic tool to assess different market situations. The other aspect to understanding a market situation is to determine the brand's market share. Understanding the market share dynamics can be a key factor in how you may approach a market. For example, let's look at the Dallas/Ft. Worth example for picante sauce. Based on its brand and category strength, Dallas/Ft. Worth should be a great growth opportunity market. What if your brand had 70 percent of the picante sauce category market share? Would this market still be a great opportunity? Or what if it had just 20 percent of the Dallas/Ft. Worth picante sauce market? Would that be a better opportunity? The answer to the latter question is a resounding "yes." Certainly, the brand would have much more upside potential if it had only 20 percent of the market compared to 70 percent of the market. Market share does provide a gauge on the potential for the brand in the market. Basically, market share tells you how much of the pie you have and how much is available. Market share offers another layer of information that helps clarify the brand's market opportunity.

Market share by itself can be misleading. You need to drill into the composition of the market to truly understand the opportunity. Figure 7.2 provides two different competitive scenarios for the Dallas/Ft. Worth picante sauce example. In both cases, your brand has a 20 percent market share. We have already established that the 20 percent market share number means that there is plenty of upside for the brand in this market.

In Scenario A, the composition of the market is highly competitive with three other brands compromising 55 percent of the market and the store brands with another 25 percent. Scenario B, however, shows that the store brands have 70 percent of the market with just one other brand with 10 percent of the market. Which scenario would best provide your

Figure 7.2
Market Share Composition Scenarios
Picante Sauce Market
Dallas/Ft. Worth

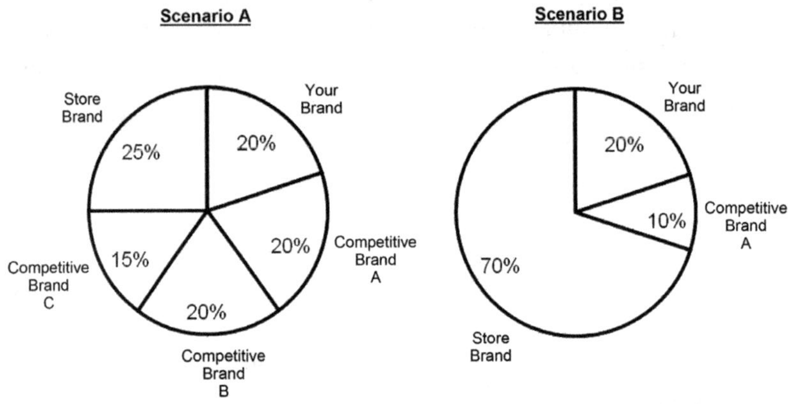

brand the greatest growth potential? Scenario A is highly competitive with no clear dominant position. Scenario B shows that the store brands totally dominate this category. Since the store brands typically make more money for the retailer and provide a price break to the consumer, gaining traction in Scenario B is going to be tough. Any upside potential here is based on taking market share from one lone brand with an outside chance of taking market share from the store or private label brand. Scenario A poses a much better prospect with 55 percent of the market held by other brands compared to just 10 percent for Scenario B.

The point is that when strategically evaluating where to best allocate your resources, digging deep into the market will help uncover the opportunity. That means evaluating the strength of the brand and the business plus the composition of the market.

Distribution plays the other role in assessing market potential. As we previously discussed, not having full distribution can negatively impact the brand's true market potential. In assessing any market situation, it is important to understand the level of distribution that the brand has attained. If it is a grocery product, then being in all the grocery stores in the market is important. Being in half of the stores can negatively impact the brand's opportunity to develop a cost effective communication plan.

Using communication to impact brand distribution can become a key strategic use of the brand's communication resources. For example, you could develop a communication plan to help gain distribution at a particular retailer. The entire plan is devoted to promoting the retailer as well as your brand. The sales force can use this as one of their primary selling points to gain shelf space for the brand.

Communication can lead the way to create a new point of distribution. For example, communication can be used to create a Direct-to-Consumer distribution model. Brands are using this approach whether it is through direct response television or just selling their brand on the web to stimulate demand. Broadcast, digital, and social media channels can all become sales channels depending upon the brand and its audience.

Analyzing Seasonality and Timing Opportunities

When to advertise is as important as where to advertise. Seasonal and specific timing opportunities can greatly impact the brand's growth.

The place to start is by understanding when your brand is purchased and how that compares to the category. To analyze seasonal opportunities, you can assess the monthly sales of your brand versus that of the category. This provides a method to assess strengths and weaknesses of seasonal sales opportunities.

Figure 7.3 is an analysis of the carbonated beverage category and a fictitious brand, PopUp. To create this sales index analysis, monthly sales for the brand and category were divided by the average sales per month and then multiplied by 100. For example, the PopUp sales index for January is 83. The index was developed through this formula (6.9 percent sales/8.3 × 100= 83).

When you review Figure 7.3, you will notice that both category and PopUp sales are the strongest from April through August. When you dig a bit deeper, you see that PopUp sales for the core months of June through August are stronger than the category. In fact, approximately one-third of PopUp's sales are concentrated in those three months. PopUp underperforms the category in the months leading into June. Perhaps there is an opportunity for PopUp to gain more sales leading into the core selling season.

Figure 7.3
Monthly Sales Analysis Example

Month	Category % Sales	Category Index	PopUp % Sales	PopUp Index
1. January	7.6	91	6.9	83
2. February	7.9	95	7.5	90
3. March	8.3	100	7.8	94
4. April	8.5	102	7.9	95
5. May	8.7	105	8.3	100
6. June	9.5	114	10.5	127
7. July	9.9	119	11.0	133
8. August	9.5	114	10.5	127
9. September	8.1	98	8.1	98
10. October	7.9	95	7.7	93
11. November	7.2	87	7.2	87
12. December	6.9	83	6.6	80

On the surface, this monthly sales analysis confirms the obvious. Summertime has the highest sales for carbonated beverages. When the temperature goes up, so does the need to drink. There are other times that stimulate the need to grab a soft drink. Some of them include eating a meal, taking a break, or needing a boost in the day.

The point is that there are natural times of the year or times of the week or day when consumers either need or buy your brand. For food and beverage brands, it begins with something as fundamental as when you are hungry or thirsty. For other brands, the purchase decision may be tied to a life event such as getting married or having a baby. Or it can be tied to category sales events around holidays. Understanding the seasonal and timing patterns for your brand as it relates to other brands within your category provides a foundation to develop strategy.

Economics of Place and Time

Geography and seasonality also have an impact on the economics of media costs. Understanding the economics helps ensure that you maximize your brand's communication resources.

Geography plays a large role in the economics of media. There are economies of scale when you move from advertising locally to nationally. This is particularly true when you advertise on national broadcasts and in national publications.

According to Nielsen, there are 210 television markets in the United States. The top 10 markets represent approximately 30 percent of the population while the top 50 markets represent approximately 66 percent of the population.

If your brand is in the top 10 markets, it may be more cost efficient to purchase national cable and/or print than to purchase each local market. This percentage where it is more cost efficient to purchase national rather than local markets is sometimes called the "national/local break-even point."

The rule of thumb when network television is more cost efficient than its local counterpart is when the brand is available in approximately 66 percent of the United States. So, if the brand is in the top 50 markets, it makes more economic sense to purchase network television than local time in those markets.

One way to look at this analysis is when you buy national cable or print, you are getting nearly 70 percent of the population for free. In the network television example, you may be getting markets 51–210 for free. That is a lot for free.

The counter-argument is that by purchasing national media, you are wasting coverage by directing your message to consumers who may not be able to buy your brand. That argument was much more valid 15 or 20 years ago (pre-Internet) when goods were largely sold in physical stores. In today's economy, the vast majority of goods can be accessible through a wide variety of channels. If this is the case with your brand, then you should certainly consider national versus local advertising.

The time of the year also has an economic impact on media costs. Just as there are natural seasonal consumer behavior patterns, there are natural patterns of advertising. The second quarter and fourth quarter of the calendar year are the strongest seasonal periods of advertising. Traditionally, January has the least advertising demand.

Paid media like any other commodity is subject to supply and demand pricing. It should come as no surprise that media companies charge more for their inventory when demand is high and less when demand is low. That is why media costs, particularly for broadcast, are the highest in the second and fourth quarters that correspond to high demand. In fact, the fourth quarter may cost 15 percent to 20 percent more than the annual average. Conversely, the first quarter may cost 15 percent less than average. By shifting media dollars from one quarter to another, the brand can potentially save significant dollars.

Because media inventory is much like a hotel room or airline seat, it can pay to be flexible. In travel, if you are flexible about when and where you go, you can sometimes get super bargain rates. The same is true in media. If you are flexible about when and where your advertising is scheduled, you can sometimes get costs that are as low as 20 cents on the dollar.

Of course, if you have a campaign that is directing consumers to a limited time offer, it makes no sense to run outside the offer window. If you are marketing a product that is used all the time such as toothpaste, being flexible may be a strategy to consider.

When approaching the strategic use of place and time, it is important to consider the economic elements of each. There are economic implications to where and when you schedule advertising. By adjusting your approach, there is the potential to greatly impact the brand's communication resources.

Strategic and Tactical Place and Time Approaches

While brand communication strategies and tactics are highly situational, they revolve around the following two themes:

- Analyzing the marketing communication opportunity.
- Analyzing the consumer relevancy opportunity.

These two themes are strategic paths to growing the brand. Both rely on insights to break from conventional place or time category patterns. Let's look at both place and time within the context of these two themes.

From a geographic perspective, the initial BDI and CDI analysis forms the bedrock for discovering the marketing opportunity. The markets that present the best opportunity are those where the brand is currently strong (BDI > 120) and the category is even stronger (CDI > BDI). This represents a true geographic or market opportunity. By applying the market share and distribution factors to the BDI/CDI analysis, you can certainly determine the best markets to apply the greatest amount of brand communication.

Strategically, this is looking for Brand Opportunity Index markets or BOI. The BOI is the result of calculating the upside potential between the BDI and CDI. For example, if Des Moines has a BDI of 120 and a CDI of 150, it has a BOI of 125. The formula for this equation is (CDI/BDI × 100 = BOI) or in this case 150/120 × 100 = 125.

Tactically, you can apply this same analysis to smaller geographical areas such as neighborhoods or even block groups. Such an analysis may reveal that the market for your brand is concentrated in just a few zip codes. Knowing this can provide leverage for the brand's communication budget. Rather than allocating dollars across an entire market, you may be able to significantly increase the impact of those dollars when geographically focused.

While the Brand Opportunity Index is a strong analytical tool that provides direction on where to best allocate the brand communication resources, there are even stronger opportunities in the area of consumer relevancy.

In this case, we are looking at geography or place through the consumer lens. The goal is to find the most relevant place(s) to communicate our brand message. For example, 60 percent of grocery brand decisions are made in store and not before the shopping trip. Based on this insight, you can conclude that placing ads in-store would be a good idea. Intercepting the consumer right at the place of purchase can be a great strategy.

Consider how you feel when you are at home versus when you are at work or commuting to work. There are places where some messages are more relevant than others. Home furnishings are a natural fit for home magazines that are read in the home. Business messages are most relevant when you are in a business environment. This is pretty much common sense.

Wisk laundry detergent applied this type of thinking to promoting their brand. Wisk is dwarfed in the laundry detergent category by some very large brands that outspend Wisk more than 10 to 1. Wisk couldn't outspend their competition but they could outthink them. The question was how to get their message to moms with grade school-age children who are constantly getting dirty. The solution was simple yet elegant. They placed their advertising where children are most likely to get dirty. The idea behind Wisk's campaign was to find "the point of dirt." So, soccer, football, softball, and baseball fields became key places for Wisk to advertise. So did playgrounds and parks. Wisk also promoted their brand at laundromats near these key "dirty destinations." Wisk took this approach one step further by encouraging children to "get dirty." They extended their idea to tap into the need for children to get outside and play.

Finding places that are relevant to the brand's communication can become a powerful strategic tool. In the pre-smartphone era, the key place to own in the home for pizza delivery services was the refrigerator. The goal was to get a refrigerator magnet with the pizza delivery service's phone number on every refrigerator in the market. Now that same idea has morphed to having the pizza delivery service app on every smartphone. Owning a place such as the top app on a smartphone can become a huge strategic advantage for the brand.

From a seasonality or time perspective, the first analysis is to determine when your brand is being purchased. Just like applying a BDI or CDI to determine market strength, you can develop a seasonal index to better understand your brand and the category.

Once you determine a sales pattern, you can then look at the communication spending pattern. Communication and specifically paid advertising typically chases sales. If December traditionally has represented 25 percent of sales, then you will see advertisers spending around 25 percent of their budget that month. Once you know the sales pattern and the spending pattern, you can determine your strategy.

Advertising in the top sales weeks or months of the year is often called "fish when the fish are biting." The challenge is that everyone has their line in the water at the same time. So, the person with the most lines in the water usually wins. In the case of advertising, this means that the advertiser that has the greatest share of spending wins. Everyone is fighting for the same consumer at the same time. It can become a very expensive proposition to continually try to outshout your competition.

This is why you see advertisers placing their advertising before the key sales period. This is called leading into the season. Basically, you are hoping to cast the first line in the water. This can be a very effective strategy particularly if the brand message is a compelling, limited time only offer. By leading into the season, your brand can stand out from the competition and begin converting consumers into sales.

Tactically, this same sales or purchase analysis can be done by week, day, and even down to the minute. This offers the opportunity to present your message at nearly the exact moment that a consumer may be in the market. That is why fast food restaurants cluster radio commercials around noon to drive their lunchtime business or between 3 p.m. and 5 p.m. for after-school snacks. Just like geography, the more tailored the time placement, the greater opportunity for effectiveness.

Finding the most relevant time to advertise can come through purchase analysis. It can also come through looking at your brand from the consumer's perspective. For example, the time of day and day of the week can greatly impact your mood and receptivity to a message. For example, most people have an afternoon slump from 2 p.m. until 4 p.m. It may not be surprising that the peak click through rate time on Facebook is 3 p.m. on Wednesday. People hit that mid-afternoon slump, check their Facebook page, and find something of interest.

Tactically, timing can be used to help make your brand relevant. From holidays to "commercial themed months," there are opportunities to tie your brand into some seasonal event or pattern. Whether it is St. Patrick's Day, Cinco de Mayo or Frozen Food month, there is always something going on that may be a brand opportunity.

Some of these days present brands with an opportunity to have fun and become a part of popular culture. April Fool's Day is one of those opportunities. In 2013, Scope "launched" a bacon-flavored mouthwash complete with a dedicated website and social media promotion. Many years before this prank, Taco Bell announced that they were buying the Liberty Bell and renaming it the Taco Bell Liberty Bell. This generated a lot of buzz even in an era before social media.

Place and time present tremendous brand communication strategic opportunities. To capitalize on these opportunities requires market analysis and consumer insight. What you hope to discover is that moment of truth when the consumer is making that purchase decision with your message front and center.

Summary

In summary, place and time form two of the three key strategic levers for any brand communication program. Coupling place and time with the target market, these represent the who, where, and when aspects of brand communication planning.

To determine the best place to advertise, brand communication professionals review the strength of the brand compared to the strength of the category on a market-by-market basis. The brand strength is called BDI which stands for Brand Development Index while the CDI stands for Category Development Index. Together these analyses show the per capita sales strength of a market. Based on this analysis, markets can be grouped into four quadrants: Star, Question Mark, Cash Cow, and Dogs. The Star represents markets where both the BDI and CDI are strong. Question Mark represents markets where CDI is strong yet the BDI is weak. These markets have potential but require more in-depth analysis. Cash Cow and Dog markets represent situations where both the BDI and CDI are under-developed.

The next phase of understanding market dynamics is to dig deeper into the distribution and market share of the brand. These factors will help to determine the true potential of the market.

Just like geography, seasonality or timing represents a strategic opportunity. To better understand this opportunity, monthly, weekly, or even daily brand and category sales analysis can be developed. Overlaying competitive spending patterns on top of this sales analysis helps to inform the brand communication professional about seasonal or timing opportunities.

Both geography and seasonality provide the brand with economic opportunities to increase the exposure of the paid media budget. The national to local market break-even point for broadcast and print media represents where purchasing national media is much more cost efficient than buying many local markets. For some media such as cable television, this break-even point can be when the brand is available in one-third of the United States.

There is seasonal supply and demand of media time/space that offers economies. When demand for advertising is historically low such as the first and third calendar quarters of the year, advertising rates are relatively low. Conversely, purchasing advertising during the fourth quarter can be quite expensive.

Strategies for place and time revolve around two themes. The first theme is to use analysis tools to determine geographical and seasonal times that provide the brand with opportunity. These opportunities are driven by market analysis. The second theme is to determine the most relevant times and places to intercept the consumer with the brand's message. Consumer insight drives these opportunities.

Place and time offer the brand a tremendous opportunity to gain a strategic advantage in the marketplace. Rigorous analysis and consumer insight provide the tools to impact the strategic approach to these two crucial areas.

Review Questions

1. What is the definition of a Brand Development Index and a Category Development Index?
2. What are the ways a BDI and CDI are used to assess geographic opportunity?
3. What factors beyond BDI and CDI are used to assess market opportunity?
4. What is the seasonality equivalent of a BDI?
5. What are the economics of national versus local market geographical distribution from a media perspective?
6. What times of the year have the greatest and least demand for advertising? How does this supply and demand cycle factor into media pricing?
7. What are the two key strategic themes for place and time?

Discussion Questions

1. What are some examples of brands with either geographic or seasonal strategies that you believe have been most effective? Why do you think they were effective?
2. How would you approach identifying geographical and seasonal strategies for a new self-driving car? What would be places and/or times that would be the most relevant for this type of product?
3. How do geographic and seasonal strategies differ for brands

that have the greatest amount of monetary resources and those that are greatly outspent in the category?

Additional Resources

Kelley, L., D. Jugenheimer, and K. Sheehan. 2015. *Advertising Media Planning: A Brand Management Approach*. 4th ed. New York: Routledge.

Kelley, L., D. Jugenheimer, and K. Sheehan. 2015. *Advertising Media Workbook and Sourcebook*. 4th ed. New York: Routledge.

Chapter 8

Developing the Strategic Idea

Learning Objectives

This chapter is intended to help you:

- Understand Maslow's Hierarchy of Needs as it relates to brand message strategy
- Understand how to establish a more nuanced knowledge of competitors
- Understand how different brands address similar problems with unique solutions

In Chapter 2, we presented the idea that brands are constantly evolving and are multilayered. Brands are part of larger categories and these categories exist in a larger world. The ideas presented in the preceding chapters helped you gather information about a brand's position in its category to start to identify a strong strategic idea. As a reminder, these three questions must be answered as the first step in creating a strategic idea:

1) Where are we today?
2) Where do we want to be?
3) How are we going to get there?

These questions require a deep dive into the brand and the category, as well as an assessment of the larger outside forces happening today.

A First Step: Meet Maslow

Abraham Maslow first presented his theory of human motivation in 1943 and it resonates with marketers and advertisers today. Maslow suggested

Figure 8.1
Maslow's Hierarchy of Needs

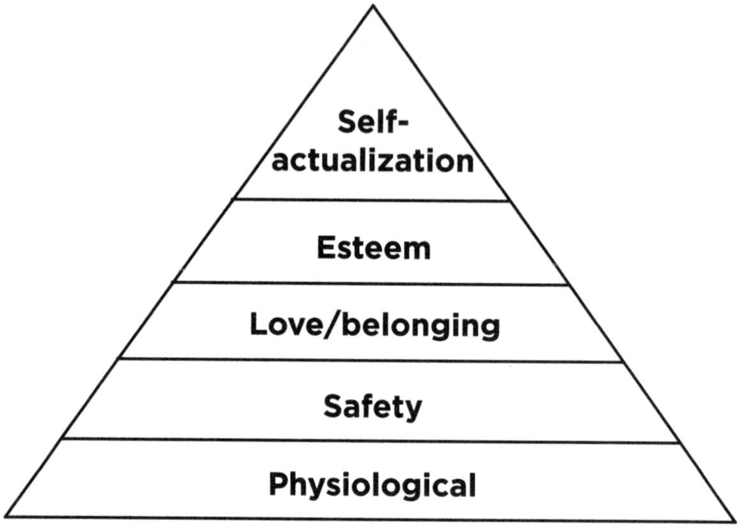

that all humans move through five stages throughout their life. These stages reflect their needs and are generally presented in a pyramid (Figure 8.1).

The most basic needs are physiological; the physical things we need to survive. Such needs include air, water, and food; for without these the body will not exist. This level also includes clothing and shelter to protect us from the elements.

The next level consists of needs about safety: personal safety, financial security, and personal health. Maslow has argued that these safety needs are particularly strong in children who have not yet learned how to fend for themselves. This need also explains the popularity of "fear appeals" as a brand strategy for products ranging from deodorant (fear of public humiliation) to home security systems (fear for personal safety).

The third level is needs related to love and belonging, and is a key strategy for many products. People need to feel a sense of belonging and acceptance among their different social groups, both in person and online. We also have an innate desire to build relationships, as cited by two researchers in what is termed the "belongingness hypothesis." Brands recognize this need and many examples exist of leveraging the use of a brand into a feeling of belonging. Harley Davidson, for example, wants its customers to feel like they are part of a group of motorcycle riders that are more closely knit than other motorcycle owners. Michelob Ultra shows us different groups of outdoor enthusiasts—the Freedom Hikers, the Open Water Paddlers—who bond over both their love of the outdoors and their love of the brand.

The fourth level is esteem: the idea that all people have a need to be respected, in terms of respect from others and self-respect. We want to be accepted and valued by others. Often this respect is gained from our profession or our participation in other activities that give people a sense of contribution or value. Dove's "Real Beauty" campaign suggests that every woman can be confident about themselves. Oprah Winfrey's ads for Weight Watchers encourage people to lose weight for themselves—not due to outside pressure (ironically, this includes advertisements suggesting we must look thin and beautiful in order to be accepted or loved).

The final level is self-actualization, which Maslow suggests is the recognition of a person's full potential and how that potential is obtained. Maslow has described this level as an individual's desire to do everything he or she can do in order to be the most he or she can be—a strategy that was used by the U.S. Army for over 20 years. This idea of self-actualization can be highly individual: for some, self-actualization might be the idea of being the ""best parent" or the "best athlete." American Express has used self-actualization in their campaigns showing how the Amex card provides people with the tools to reach their full potential, focusing on photographers Pei Ketron in Iceland and Paul Nicklen in Alaska.

It is important to note that as one moves up the hierarchy, the needs move from being more rational to being more emotional. Rarely do advertising messages suggest that the product or service is necessary for an individual to survive, yet most build on a need suggested by the hierarchy.

Competitors

As a first step, you should examine at what level you and your competitors operate. It is not necessary for every brand to be operating at a different level on the hierarchy, but the hierarchy itself can suggest some interesting strategic options to be considered. Often, brands in a single category can have the same problem (such as the need to build market share or to create a more positive image among consumers). This is especially true when there isn't a clear market leader. Brands will select different levels of the hierarchy to not only differentiate themselves from competitors but also to connect with consumers at a need level that will resonate with them.

For example, in examining the credit card category, we can see how different credit cards choose to position themselves at different levels. We have already seen that American Express focuses on self-actualization. Capital One has a family of credit cards that provide a range of benefits including unlimited miles or cash back—both focusing on safety needs (feeling safe that you have strong financial resources that can be used effectively). Visa, on the other hand, stresses the sense of belonging by saying that Visa can be used everywhere an individual wants to be.

Changes in Category Competition

It is one thing to look at a category like credit cards where very few categorical alternatives exist—what is an alternative to a credit card? Well, checks or cash exist, yet most people prefer a credit (or debit) card for its convenience and safety. However, for other categories, a broader view of the category should be undertaken. Is the category growing or has it stagnated? Why? Are there other products and other categories that are replacing the category where your brand has traditionally operated?

For example, beer companies such as Miller, Coors, and Anheuser-Busch have traditionally operated in the "macrobrew" category (made up of large breweries), and now face competition from microbrews, hard ciders, and hard lemonade. Arguably, beers can also compete with any other alcoholic beverage, or a sports drink, or even water, depending on the individual. As a result, it is necessary to track the fortunes and foibles of related categories to have the best picture of what is happening to your brand. Examining how these outside competitors position themselves using Maslow's Hierarchy of Needs is also valuable.

Outside Forces

Finally, the current status of the world must be considered. While this may seem like an overwhelming task, two questions are key: Are things stable financially? Are things stable socially? Often we find that when one area is stable, the other is in flux. If the economy is good and shows signs of improving, then social issues are often more of a concern. If the economy is bad, this becomes more important to many people than social issues.

When the economy is good, people are making purchases but in general not worrying too much about the economic situation. When the economy is bad, though, people cut back on purchases, trade down to generic or lower-cost options, and go out less. We can also consider aspects of the "attention economy" for analyzing this further. The idea of an attention economy suggests that people have a finite amount of attention—that is, the ability to focus their energies on a particular item of information and decide whether to act on the information or not. When the economy is good, we have to spend less of our time worrying about how to make ends meet and can devote more time to the bigger social problems in the world. When the economy is bad, we revert to the second level of Maslow's Hierarchy—the safety level—to make sure that we are financially safe in bad times.

Advertising's Role in Problem-Solving

The two previous sections suggest that the environment in which advertising operates is always dynamic: people are changing, their wants and needs are changing, and the competitive landscape is changing. Where people find themselves on the hierarchy of needs is also in flux. The ultimate challenge for brands is to identify what is the real problem that consumers have, and to then identify whether brand communication can solve the problem.

One good place to start is with the brand's mission statement. The mission statement for Coca-Cola, for example, reads as follows:

> "At the Coca-Cola Company, we strive to refresh the world. Inspire moments of optimism and happiness, create value, and make a difference."

What consumer problem does Coca-Cola wish to solve? People are thirsty for more than something to quench their thirst: they are thirsty for happiness and inspiration. Is this a problem that can be solved with a brand message? Can a message make people feel happy and inspired whenever they open a bottle or can of Coke? Coke believes a message can help people understand the power of Coke, and thus the campaign "Open Happiness" was born.

From Brand Insights to Big Ideas

Once we understand what consumers want and need from brands, and what messages they are already hearing from similar brands, we can now begin to identify what is known as the "big idea." A big idea is distinct from other category messages and can work to change the way people view both the category and the brand. It connects with people at a deep level and can be used in all types of marketing efforts. The big idea can address emotional issues and life challenges faced by the target; some of these issues are physical issues (such as needs to be healthier) and others address psychological issues (such as the need to feel beautiful, or cool, or safe). You will notice, of course, that these issues all relate back to Maslow.

Nicorette gum is one of many products that help people quit smoking. Many products in this category use guilt and fear appeals to motivate people to quit (recognizing for example that many people try to quit multiple times), and review the variety of health reasons to quit. However, Nicorette recognized that people knew all the rational reasons to quit and often chose not to; as a result, Nicorette addressed a key emotional insight in their advertising: that quitting is hard. Their big idea is: "Quitting sucks. Nicorette makes quitting suck less."

Dove went through a similar process when they examined all the competitive advertising promising women that different products would make them beautiful and conducted an extensive global research study. The competitive ads and the research both pointed to the fact that society's definition of beauty had become at best limiting and at worst unattainable. Indeed, the research showed that only 2 percent of women considered themselves beautiful. Dove's response was the big idea that "women are naturally beautiful" and the resulting campaign was the famous "Real Beauty" campaign.

What do these big idea statements have in common? First, they both state truths that consumers can relate to, but perhaps never hear in their day to day lives. They both have the ability to change some specific attitudes (such as "I will never be able to quit" or "I will never be beautiful"). They are simple statements but are both novel in that they encompass messages that we generally don't hear about in the advertising world. They also have a degree of "magnetism"—in that people want to be pulled into the idea. They can be used in multiple types of marketing communication, and speak to consumers in the language that they can relate to. Finally, people want to relate to these brands because the brands show they relate to people.

Addressing Problems

Understanding the key problem facing the brand, the needs and wants of the target audience, the nature of its competitors, and the outside forces, can together lead to new strategic ideas. A comparison of two cases will illustrate how this works. In the 1990s, two different countries—Great Britain and New Zealand—both wanted to improve on two things: first, their attractiveness as a tourist destination and second, their value to outside investment and investors. These two countries, though, each had unique problems that had to be addressed.

Great Britain had an image of being old fashioned and stodgy. Britain's image was stuck in the past. People who had been on vacation to Britain during the 1970s and 1980s didn't think they had to return since there was nothing new to see or do. And it wasn't just tourism that was suffering; institutional investors did not see the country as progressive or innovative and weren't looking to fund businesses there.

To address this, the government sponsored a campaign to represent Great Britain (and London in particular) as modern, young, and diverse. The tagline associated with this campaign was "Cool Britannia," a play on "Rule Britannia," a British patriotic song. The "Cool Britannia" campaign was first developed in consultation with a task force of people representing both arts and technology, and that task force wanted the message to reinforce that the country was hip, enterprising, and cool, due in part to the multicultural influences of immigrants in the country. Many people felt that the campaign gave a sense of optimism to the country, and one measure of success was that *Vanity Fair* magazine devoted an entire issue to the so-called creative class in the UK. While tourism dollars increased during the campaign period (1996–1998), "Cool Britannia" did not resonate with internal audiences (citizens of Great Britain) because many felt alienated from the young creative class personified in the campaign. This reflects the need for input from all stakeholders before a campaign goes live.

New Zealand's problem was different: many people around the world had no idea of where New Zealand was and what it had to offer. New Zealand saw itself as having a unique blend of landscapes, people, and activities ranging from mountains to beaches, all in the space of a country about the size of Colorado. The connection to Māori culture is also very strong, creating a nation with a strong sense of equality. Launched in 1999, their campaign theme was "100 percent Pure New Zealand" which communicates how the country's unique combination of landscapes, people, and activities cannot be found anywhere else in the world. Traveling to New Zealand is a "100 percent Pure New Zealand" visitor experience.

Over the years the campaign theme has been extended into other related themes such as 100 percent Pure Relaxation, 100 percent Pure Welcome, 100 percent Pure Adrenalin, and 100 percent Pure You—all connected back to the core premise of 100 percent Pure New Zealand. Most recently, the campaign features the theme "100 percent Middle-Earth" leveraging the exposure New Zealand attained around the world from the "Hobbit" movies. The "100 percent Pure" campaign, with all its appropriate evolutions, is still working successfully today.

Summary

This chapter introduced Maslow's Hierarchy of Needs as a way to stimulate the development of the strategic idea. Considering all aspects of a brand, including competition and key outside forces affecting the brand, all play into the development of a strategic idea. The chapter also indicated why input from multiple stakeholders is necessary to develop a brand message that will last.

Review Questions

1. What was Maslow attempting to do when he developed the Hierarchy of Needs?
2. What are the five levels of Maslow's Hierarchy of Needs?
3. What does the state of the economy have to do with brands?
4. Why is New Zealand's campaign successful but Great Britain's campaign unsuccessful?

Discussion Questions

1. Find three or four ads from the recent Super Bowl broadcast. Where would these fall on Maslow's Hierarchy? If you notice any patterns, why do you think those patterns occurred?
2. In good economic times, people are devoting more attention to noneconomic issues (e.g., social issues). What should brands do regarding their involvement in social issues? Is a strategy addressing a brand's relationship to social issues a good strategy? Discuss the pros and cons of such.
3. Have you seen any other examples of countries promoting themselves? Where do their messages fall on the Hierarchy of Needs? What specific problems do these messages seem to be addressing? Do they do a good job?

Additional Resources

Dinnie, K. 2008. Nation *Branding: Concepts, Issues, Practice*. New York: Taylor & Francis.

Maslow, A. H. 1998. *Maslow on Management*. New York: John Wiley & Sons.

New Zealand Tourism Board. n.d. Official Website. Available at http://www.newzealand.com/us/.

Werther, C. 2011. Rebranding Britain: Cool Britannia, the Millennium Dome and the 2012 Olympics. *Moderna språk, 105* (1): 1–14.

Chapter 9

Communication Strategy

Learning Objectives

This chapter is intended to help you:

- Understand the current landscape in light of how it effects strategy development
- Understand the specific components of a communication strategy and how they are created
- Examine how agency structure can influence the development of the strategy

The Current Landscape

Brands are evolving, to be sure, but other things change as well. What is clear is that the current communications landscape is also evolving. Where marketers and advertisers used to have a few basic decisions to make—TV or radio, newspapers or magazines—we are now faced with many more nuanced decisions to make. Some of the key changes in the landscape to remember are:

- Marketing messages now make up the majority of the noise surrounding people every day—from ads in traditional media to branded content to sponsored events to live brand experiences; many facets of life have become opportunities to deliver messages to audiences.
- Media is more fragmented than ever before. Reaching a "mass" audience is harder than ever.
- The Internet provides a multitude of new possibilities for communicating messages. At the same time, it has fragmented the attention of consumers to a great degree.

- The boundaries separating consumers and brands have become incredibly fluid. Consumers no longer only receive content from brands, they now contribute content to brands and remix branded content for their own purposes.

The communications strategy is the plan on how brand goals will be met. At the same time, today's communication strategy must contain a holistic approach to engage an audience around a message. This is the essence of the 360 degree approach: instead of examining each communication opportunity on its own discrete strengths and weaknesses, all methods must be considered in terms of how they integrate with one another. Every channel is a possible route to a consumer, and every channel is not necessarily a paid channel.

From Big Idea to Communications Strategy

Chapter 8 discussed various ways to develop a big idea. Having a big idea is key in order to make sure the message is heard loud and clear across the various channels that the message strategy must employ. And the big idea must be so interesting that customers can't resist the idea, and that the advertising creative and other message crafters are inspired to create great work surrounding the idea.

The big idea is internal: it is used by everyone involved with the brand to make sure all aspects of the brand will be clear (unique from other brands), consistent (across different platforms), and constant (visible in the marketplace). The big idea is translated into external communications campaigns through the communication strategy.

Consumers have the opportunity to connect and interact with brands in many ways, and so the translation of the big idea into the communication strategy must recognize this opportunity to provide multiple touch points and experiences with the brand. The big idea will then be integrated into all aspects of the communication strategy.

The big idea also helps inform media and channel selection. Multiple channels can reach many in the target audience, but the key strategic idea may only be appropriate for a subset of those channels. For example, for a cell phone company, there are numerous ways to communicate strength of coverage, but one of the most popular ways is with a visual map. It could arguably be more effective to do comparisons of our brand with other brands using some type of visual information. As a result, certain channels are likely to be eliminated.

Components of a Communication Strategy

Communication strategies tend to have a consistent set of components listed below. We will discuss each of these in turn.

- An objective
- A budget
- Targeting
- A strategic idea
- Channel choices and measurement
- Integration

Setting Objectives

The starting point for a communication objective is the overall business objective of the brand. And the starting point for the business objective is identifying the key problems facing the brand, as we discussed in Chapter 3. The communication objective should help contribute to the overall goals of the brand. In this way, the communication program is not seen as an "add-on" program but as an integral part of the brand and fundamental to the success of the organization.

Table 9.1 compares how brand objectives and communication objectives relate for a fictional cell phone service called "AllCell." This brand recognizes that increasing numbers of people are getting rid of their landlines and using only cell phones for communication. It has also done research saying that many cell phone users believe all cell phone companies are basically alike—and none of them are very good. Thus, customers are willing to change for an easily attainable low rate. As a result, the brand has set goals to differentiate itself from competitors through coverage and customer service in the year to come. The big idea is that AllCell is the only company providing superior connections both in terms of coverage (customers are connected to their networks) and customer service (customers are connected to the company).

Next is how the brand objectives might translate to communication objectives.

Table 9.1
The Relationship between Brand Objectives and Communication Objectives

	Brand Objective	Communication Objective
Brand elements	To increase coverage to 95% of the United States	Create awareness of our coverage strength relative to competitors among 85% of customers over the next six months
Customers	To provide optimal customer service to all clients	Create knowledge of awards won in customer service area among all consumers over the next year
	To increase customer retention by 10% by offering a loyalty program	Create desire to continue with the service among 30% of consumers
		Increase engagement and interactions on key social media channels with 25% more interactions per week
Employees	Increase employee satisfaction with the company by 15%	Create awareness of new channels for interactions so employees know they are heard and supported
		Create awareness of protocols for employee engagement on social media to implement in next three months

Objectives should be assessed using the SMART acronym: each objective must be specific, measurable, attainable, relevant, and time bound. Take the first communication objective: "Create awareness of our coverage strength relative to competitors among 85 percent of customers over the next six months."

- Is the objective specific? Yes, since it names a specific brand attribute (coverage strength) to be used in the messaging.
- Is it measurable? Yes, since it provides a numeric goal to be achieved.
- Is it attainable? Probably. It is a fairly simple message that with smart targeting should be attainable. If the goal was set at 100 percent, in contrast, we could argue that it would not be attainable.
- Is it relevant? Yes, since according to the brand's proprietary research customers want to know their service is available everywhere they go, and many competitors cannot guarantee that.
- Is it time bound? Yes, as there is a date specified as to when the goal should be reached.

What is important to note is that these objectives are tied into changes and improvements that are outside the responsibility of the communications team yet key to the success of the communications effort. A good brand manager must keep in touch with the other people in the organization to make sure that the brand is moving forward.

Developing the Budget

Chapter 5 provides guidance on developing a budget strategy. What is important is that the budget is sufficient to meet the goals. This seems like a fairly straightforward idea but is often overlooked. Take the first objective. The media strategists should be able to provide an estimate on how much it would cost to create awareness among 85 percent of existing customers. If that budget is not available, the goal might be revised to create awareness among 70 or 75 percent of customers.

It is also important to note that some of these objectives are more difficult to achieve than others—and thus will require more resources. The general rule of thumb is that it is easiest to develop awareness, a bit more difficult to develop interest or knowledge, and even more difficult to create desire or an emotional connection to the brand.

There also needs to be a discussion of the relative priorities of the communication objectives. For our fictional company, there are six different objectives, and each one may not be equally as important to various stakeholders in the company. Jointly deciding on priorities will help allocate budgets more effectively.

Targeting

We discussed the basics of targeting strategy in Chapter 6. For the communications strategy, having the most rich and vivid description of the audience makes it easier to construct an effective communication strategy for them. Often we stop at demographic descriptors of target audiences when we should think a bit deeper about them. For our fictional cell phone company, then, we could ask:

- Are our target customers opinion leaders or opinion followers? Which of our customers have influence over others and which are looking for opinion leaders to help them make decisions? How do opinion leaders make choices? How do opinion followers decide who to listen to?
- Are our target customers light, medium, or heavy users of cell phones? Do they have a landline or not? Do they rely on the service primarily for calls, or are they using their cell phones for other types of communications?
- Are our target customers frequent switchers or do they have the potential to be loyal? Are they considered loyal because they are simply too lazy to switch or do they truly have a strong affinity for our company?
- What else do we know about our target audience's lifestyle? How many devices do they own? How much time do they spend communicating digitally? How important is a company's association with charitable causes? That a company is a green company?

Key Strategic Idea

When looking at our fictional cell phone brand, we have identified two themes that arise from the attributes connected to coverage and customer service: strength and connection. Our first step would be to examine the competitive landscape to see if other brands are using either of these themes in their messaging. Then, we can use Maslow's Hierarchy of Needs (see Chapter 8) to identify some options for the idea, as described in Table 9.2.

Table 9.2
Developing Strategies Based on Maslow for "AllCell"

	Strength	Connection
Physiological	Only the strong survive	There's someone there for you
Safety	Never lose a call	Always be connected
Belonging	Be part of the group that is #1	Never be disconnected
Esteem	People want to be part of your group	We are always there for you
Self-actualization	Only the strong survive	I am always there

Channel Choices

As we mentioned at the start of this chapter, the communications landscape has greatly changed in the past few years. The greatest changes have arguably happened within the area of media and channels. This is important to highlight since your clients may have a different view of channels and media than you have—they may not be as informed and up-to-date as you are. As a result, you should lead a discussion highlighting some of the key choices that must be made given the new channel landscape:

- What is the right balance of paid, free, and earned media? It is important the communications strategy consider not only paid channels but also sources related to public relations and promotion. The role and importance of user-generated content should also be addressed.
- What is the right mix of "one-way" versus "two-way"? This is related in some ways to the first bullet point but focuses more on where the brand is willing to put in the effort—how much time and energy can the brand give to two-way communication to engage audiences?
- Should you go "broad and shallow" or "narrow and deep"? A traditional campaign using television is seen as "broad and shallow" meaning it is possible to reach a lot of people with a

fairly simple message. An alternative today is to go "narrow and deep"—that is, to create engagement with a smaller group of people—perhaps opinion leaders for your brand. Most brands will want some mix and balance of the two.

- How much is too much? How many is too many? Your brand can never be present in every channel that every consumer is using. Selectivity of channel is more important than ever and examining each channel's strength in meeting the objective is a priority for the marketing team.
- How to measure exposure versus engagement? Chapter 18 will discuss how to measure success, but it is important at this point to recognize that the concepts of exposure and engagement are two very different things. Just because a message is exposed to 85 percent of your audience does not mean that they will retain any of the message the first, second, or tenth time that they see or hear it. Understanding ways to measure consumer response and engagement is key to determining success.

Integration

In the new media landscape, it is highly important that the channels you select for your communication plan all work together. Each channel should have a specific role in achieving some or all of a specific objective. Each channel should also be more effective because of the presence of the message in other channels—the same message in one channel can serve sometimes as an awareness message or sometimes as a reminder message, depending on when in the campaign the message airs.

A simple way to consider integration is to think of ads for the Super Bowl and the relatively new practice of brands launching "teaser ads" in social media like YouTube and Facebook for several weeks before the game. The ads on social media give a sneak peak to the actual ads airing during the game. Consumers may be "on the lookout" for the ads during the game and already have some idea of the storyline so the "payoff" can be more impactful.

In this example, the executions were similar but not exactly the same. They are using the same creative idea without necessarily sharing all the same imagery or verbiage. Ultimately, having a consistent creative idea will help guarantee integration across channels.

Who Leads the Process?

Communication strategy begins with the client and the client's identification of the overall business goals for the brand. After that, though, there are several paths that can be taken to develop the strategy.

The **client-led model** starts with the assumption that the client holds all the important knowledge about the brand. The client then does the strategic thinking on their own, and agencies are asked to execute in the channels that are needed. This puts all the accountability on the client side.

The **lead-agency model** recognizes that agencies can bring significant expertise to the strategy table as the client choses one particular agency with the responsibility of creating the communication strategy. Some clients have multiple ad agencies, and most clients have separate advertising and PR agencies (and perhaps a separate sales promotion agency). Choosing one agency provides a focus and a leadership responsibility for one agency. Other agencies then execute the plan.

The **all -agency model** brings together representatives from all the client's agencies to create the strategy together for the benefit of the brand. This provides broader perspectives to the process.

Summary

Communications objectives are related yet distinct from marketing objectives. A good communication objective should transparently connect to the success of the marketing objective. The strategy also includes information about the target audience, the key strategic idea, and channel choices. How different media will be integrated is also important to note upfront in the strategy to make sure that this occurs throughout the campaign.

Review Questions

1. What are the key changes to the communications landscape that affect planning the communication strategy?
2. What does SMART stand for relative to communications objectives?

3. What does "broad and shallow" and "narrow and deep" refer to? Why is it important to the strategic plan?
4. What are the three process models to developing a strategic communication plan? What are the strengths and weaknesses of each?

Discussion Questions

1. How might a campaign that is "broad and shallow" differ from one that is "narrow and deep?" Think of a specific example of one or the other and discuss how it reflects one of these choices.
2. In Table 9.2, the key strategic idea for "strength" is the same for both physiological and self-actualization aspects. Why does this work?
3. The brand objectives presented for the fictitious cell phone brand AllCell included objectives for both external (consumer) and internal (employee) communication. Why is it important that employee communication be integrated with consumer communication?
4. Given what you know about the fictitious cell phone brand AllCell, which strategic idea on Table 9.2 might you recommend? Why?

Additional Resources

Lalama, M. 2015. Setting Clear Communication Objectives: A Proposed Frame of Reference to Measure the Effectiveness of Advertising and Integrated Marketing Communications Campaigns. Available at https://bit.ly/2fhw6Xo.

Stafford, A. 2012. Major Key Objectives of Marketing Communications—Explained. Available at http://www.marketingcommunicationsblog.com/Major-Key-Objectives-Of-Marketing-Communications-Explained/.

Chapter 10

Components of Brand Message Strategy

Learning Objectives

This chapter is intended to help you:

- Understand the relationship between the strategic idea and the brand message strategy
- Understand the elements of a brand message strategy
- Examine the difference between informational and transformational strategies, and know when to use each
- Think about the importance of brand personality in the brand strategy

What Is Brand Message Strategy?

A brand message strategy is a long-term strategy to support a brand, based on an understanding of the target consumers' preferences and expectations from the brand. One important aspect of the brand strategy is that it is long-term. Why? Today, many brand managers and agency account managers and planners are driven more by tactics. They want to show immediate progress toward meeting goals to show that they know what they're doing in order to leverage the brand's success into other projects for the brand (such as brand extensions) and themselves (such as job advancement). This isn't new—a reluctance to consider brands in the long term has been present for decades. It is easy for people to become focused on the best ways to manage processes given budget constraints and getting jobs done, on time, and on budget.

However, the brand message strategy is of upmost importance. It is the entire experience customers (and prospective customers) have with the brand and defines what you stand for and the personality you convey. It includes not only the logo, brand name, color palette, and slogan but also any other day-to-day interactions the brand has in the world. This includes the choices you make in all media channels, such as the images you convey, the messages that are delivered in any channel, the way employees interact with customers, and how a customer views you relative to the competitive set.

A strong brand message strategy should lead to improved:

- Brand equity: the amount of money that customers are willing to pay just because it's your brand. In addition to generating revenue, brand equity makes your company more valuable over the long term
- Brand image: how customers view the brand
- Brand value: the monetary value of a brand on a company's asset sheet
- Brand loyalty: customer commitment to your brand over time

Developing a Brand Message Strategy

A brand message strategy takes the strategic idea that was developed (see Chapter 8) and assesses how this message can be integrated into the brand so that every time a consumer sees or hears the brand, they also receive a consistent message about the brand. As a result, the message strategy becomes the foundation for every effort that is undertaken surrounding the brand.

The positioning statement is developed by evaluating your strategic idea and crafting it in a way that resonates with your target audience. At the same time, it should also resonate with other stakeholders such as employees and shareholders so they will feel positive about the brand and be able to articulate the brand message when they talk about it with other stakeholders.

One place to begin thinking about a brand message strategy is to consider a pressing problem held by the target and how the brand can help solve the problem. In general, message strategies fall into broad categories: informational and transformational.

Informational Strategies

Informational strategies solve consumer problems by providing enough information— solid facts—so that the consumer can make a rational comparison relative to competitive offerings. At the same time, a benefit should be associated with the information that is provided. One example is for the brand "Scrubbing Bubbles." "Scrubbing Bubbles" is a product line produced by SC Johnson Company that includes cleaning products for kitchens and bathrooms. The products contain ingredients that stick to surfaces and foam up so that minimal wiping or scrubbing is required. Their brand message begins with "we do the work" which captures the rational value of the product. The message ends with "so you don't have to" which presents a key consumer benefit. If I don't have to work hard to clean my kitchen, what could I do with all that time? The additional time is the key benefit that "Scrubbing Bubbles" promises me as a consumer.

The informational strategy works well in this situation for several reasons. The consumer has likely had experiences with the context: most people have had to clean their kitchen or bathroom at some point. Also, a key insight is that most people don't see cleaning their kitchen or bathroom as an enjoyable activity, yet they recognize that it is an activity that must be done. The "Scrubbing Bubbles" strategy allows consumers to make comparisons to other product offerings in the category and to choose between those products in the consideration set. A consumer may think, for example, "Does Bon Ami do the work so I don't have to? Not really. I have to scrub a bit with Bon Ami, so maybe I'll try Scrubbing Bubbles."

Transformational Strategies

Transformational strategies focus more on how the consumer will feel when they are using the brand—or to say it another way, how the brand will transform the consumer. Often, a transformational strategy is used for products considered "luxury" or "hedonic." Hedonic means "characterized by pleasure." As such, we often see transformational strategies used by brands who want to position their products as a "treat" or a "reward." In the 1970s, Miller Beer's strategy was to communicate to blue-collar workers in physically demanding jobs that Miller Beer was their "reward" for a hard day. Similarly, Breyers Gelato positions their ice cream to parents as "not for kids," suggesting a level of sophisticated indulgence that is the parent's "reward" for a hard day of parenting. For both these categories (beer and ice cream), the consumer can compare the promised experience (reward for hard work) to the experience provided by competitive brands.

Other transformational messages are used for experiences that may not have been experienced by the consumer. Resort and cruise strategic messages, for example, focus on the range of activities available for a couple or a family to feel more together or united. The message then is that the vacation can transform people into a more loving unit. Conversely, Las Vegas turned this idea of a transformational strategy on its ear with the message strategy that Las Vegas it the place where people can cut loose and enjoy themselves without consequences. This strategy connects the brand with the idea of freedom: freedom to indulge in great food and entertainment, as well as freedom from one's everyday life. This idea of freedom resulted in the famous campaign "What happens in Vegas, stays in Vegas."

Support

Message strategies also contain support points—three to four pieces of information that reinforce the importance of the key brand message. In addition, the support may also show the uniqueness of the message. Basically, support points provide reasons why consumers can believe the message strategy: they explain the positioning statement and answer key consumer questions, such as "how can the brand do that?"

How can Scrubbing Bubbles do all that work? The brand states that the product has a "foaming, grime-busting formula" that "penetrates and dissolves to help with cleaning soap scum." These support points help consumers visualize exactly how the product will act when it is used for cleaning a messy shower.

Why is Breyers Gelato an ice cream for parents, not kids? According to the brand, it is because of the sophisticated and decadent flavors (such as Tiramisu and Cappuccino Chocolate) and that each flavor contains three different textures (e.g., Tiramisu contains ladyfinger pieces and espresso sauce).

What makes Las Vegas a place for consequence-free fun? First, it is a desert city that is geographically distant from many other cities in the United States so people feel a sense of being in a completely different place than the place they came from. The wide variety of restaurants, casinos, shows, and nightlife allow people to have a range of experiences. And finally, the Vegas ethos suggests that anyone who travels there is in tacit agreement that what happens there, stays there.

Brand Personality

One way to think about your brand message strategy is to think of your brand as a person with a distinct personality. By attributing human characteristics to your brand, your brand becomes more relatable to people. The traits in a brand, like the traits in most people, remain consistent over time. Identifying a brand personality is also a good way to examine the competition and make sure your personality is unique, relevant, and able to resonate with customers.

Table 10.1
Five Major Brand Personalities

Brand Personality	Associated Traits	Example
Sincerity	Domestic, honest, genuine, cheerful, wholesome	Rachael Ray, Michelin
Excitement	Daring, spirited, imaginative, up-to-date, sensual, assertive, humorous	Burton Snowboards, Bud Light
Competence	Reliable, responsible, dependable, efficient, secure, competitive, beneficial, intelligent	Charles Schwab Brokerage, All State Insurance
Sophistication	Glamorous, pretentious, romantic, charming, rational, trustworthy, prestigious	Chanel, Dos Equis
Ruggedness	Tough, strong, outdoorsy, rugged	The North Face, Brawny Paper Towels

Some researchers argue that there are five major types of brand personalities, as outlined in Table 10.1. Using these five major personalities, a study of the brand personalities of Coke and Pepsi by Kinjal Gandhi found that consumers saw Coca-Cola as more down to earth, honest, sincere, and reliable compared to Pepsi. Pepsi was seen as more charming, outdoorsy, and cheerful. Scrubbing Bubbles, which we discussed earlier, would be seen as tough, strong, dependable, and efficient. Breyers Gelato would be glamorous, pretentious and daring. Las Vegas would use elements of excitement and sophistication in its brand personality.

You aren't stuck using only these traits though. We might describe Scrubbing Bubbles as bubbly and effervescent, and we might call Breyers Gelato sexy. Think of your brand as a person with a distinct personality. Describe him or her, then convey these traits in everything you do and create. Using the traits, choose colors, fonts, and other visual elements that match your personality. Think about ways that employees can communicate the brand personality in their work as well.

The Importance of Consistency

A good message strategy can be used consistently but should also be flexible. Aren't those two terms polar opposites? Not necessarily. The key to consistency is thinking of your brand and your brand personality and to choose what to show or tell based on whether it relates to or enhances your personality. At the same time, avoid talking about things that don't relate to or enhance your brand. Does the photo on the brand's Facebook page match your personality and align with your message? Or is it just something that someone found amusing?

Consistency leads to a cohesive message and ultimately leads to increased brand recognition, which will finally lead to brand loyalty.

Consistency sets clear standards for your brand. Flexibility allows you to make any adjustments to build interest in your brand and distinguish your brand and brand personality from your competitors. Consistency makes your brand identifiable; flexibility keeps it fresh. Some reasons why maintaining a balance between consistency and flexibility are:

1. Just as your goals in life might change over time, so might your brand goals.
2. Similarly, just as you might modify your plan to achieve your goals in life, so too might your brand marketing plan change.
3. Finally, just as you seize opportunities to move closer to your goals as they arise throughout your life, you'll also seize short-term opportunities to grow your brand and move closer to achieving your long-term brand goals as those opportunities are presented to you.

As we mentioned earlier, achieving a sense of consistency is important if you wish to build brand recognition. And while a style guide can help you achieve a cohesive digital experience, it's equally important for your employees to be well versed in the how they should be communicating with customers and representing the brand.

If your brand is playful and bubbly through Twitter engagements, then it wouldn't make sense if a customer called in and was connected with a grumpy, monotone representative, right?

This becomes challenging when brands try to "refresh" their images. A brand refresh strategy is undertaken when a brand choses to update certain elements of its image. This can include revising or updating the logo, changing color palettes, and/or bringing more consistency to different channel communications. However, the essential brand personality should remain consistent.

In 2015, Google refreshed its brand. Google's brand personality is competence: it is the first place many online users go to find information with over 40,000 different search request processes every second of every day (that is a lot of exposure to a logo!). At the same time, many users see Google as an omnipresent collector of personal information—sometimes it is possible to believe that Google knows more about us than we know about ourselves, and this puts some people off. The strategy of Google's brand refresh was to make the company more friendly and benevolent: instead of a behemoth of data, a friendly guide to the vast universe of the Internet was implied. The evolution of the Google logo can be seen at this Wikipedia site: https://en.wikipedia.org/wiki/Google_logo.

The new logo kept the familiar color palette but changed the font to a proprietary font called "Product Sans," a design that was developed to be more friendly and accessible. It also works better in mobile media. Some see the new logo as more youthful than the one it replaced, which was often referred to as quirky.

Others see it as a misstep for the brand, comparing the new logo to things like children's alphabet refrigerator magnets. The brand as personified by the old logo was a symbol of competence; the brand as personified by the new logo is less dignified, more happy-go-lucky. But given the reasons why we love the Google search engine—we trust we will find exactly what we want—this new personality seems at odds.

Evaluation

How do you know if your message strategy is a good one?

- It is adaptable: a good brand message statement can be used in all types of marketing communications such as product descriptions in catalogs, websites, sales presentations, advertisements, public relations efforts, and internal communications. The brand message should be able to be used—with minimal changes if any—to all these groups.
- It is believable: a good brand message statement will reflect the current perspectives of the target audience and address a key problem that they have.
- It is compelling: the message will provide a benefit that consumers want and have a positive reaction to.

Brand Example: Zappos

Zappos is an online retailer (purchased by Amazon in 2009) that primarily focuses on shoes but also sells several clothing lines. Zappos has been known for its fast shipping and good customer service. But their brand is so much more. In 2009, Zappo's CEO Tony Hsieh wrote this on his blog:

> "At Zappos, our belief is that if you get the culture right, most of the other stuff—like great customer service, or building a great long-term brand, or passionate employees and customers—will happen naturally on its own. We believe that your company's culture and your company's brand are really just two sides of the same coin. The brand may lag the culture at first, but eventually it will catch up. Your culture is your brand. So how do you build and maintain the culture that you want?"

Hsieh goes on to say that the culture (and thus the brand) is built through hiring people that reflect the brand: they look for people who are "adventurous, creative, fun and open-minded" and are also "passionate, determined, and humble." Those words can also clearly describe a brand. New employee training shows all employees how to be ambassadors for the brand and to provide the best customer service in the world.

If you've ever had a problem with a pair of shoes purchased from Zappos, you know that they send out replacements immediately—often overnight. Their free return policy also allows customers to order several different sizes to make sure the shoes fit right. But the website "Zappos Insights" shows other ways that brand lives up to its culture:

- Zappos paid tolls for all drivers on a particular stretch of the Massachusetts Turnpike during the Thanksgiving holiday. They wanted to reduce stress for drivers during the holiday. Does that have anything to do with shoes? No. But it has everything to do with caring about people, and it is a quirky way to show it—somewhat like Zappos itself.
- A Zappos customer bought six pairs of shoes for her mother, who had a recent medical treatment that left her foot sore and sensitive to pressure. Unfortunately, none of the pairs worked for the customer's mom, and she returned them. Two days later, the mother received a huge bouquet of flowers and a get-well-soon message from Zappos, and all family members were upgraded to VIP membership.

The bottom line is Zappos' key strategic idea is to "deliver happiness"—and that is reflected in all aspects of its activities and brand messages.

Summary

A brand message strategy is important to build value for the brand. Brand strategies can be primarily informational or transformational. The brand message strategy consists of a key strategic idea as well as support for the idea so that the idea is believable and compelling.

Review Questions

1. What are brand loyalty, brand value, brand equity, and brand image? How does the brand message strategy contribute to both?
2. What are the differences between the strategy and the support?
3. What is the difference between informational and transformational strategies?

Discussion Questions

1. Identify a brand message strategy that is adaptable. Why do you think it is adaptable? How might this strategy look if it wasn't an adaptable strategy? Are there times when an adaptable strategy should be used?
2. Identify a brand message strategy that you think is transformational. Why do you think it is transformational? What would it look like if it was informational?
3. What are some ways to find out if your brand message strategy is believable and compelling?

Additional Resources

Aaker, J. 1997. *Dimensions of Brand Personality*. Available at https://faculty-gsb.stanford.edu/aaker/PDF/Dimensions_of_Brand_Personality.pdf.

Gandhi, K. 2014. A Study of Brand Personality of Coca Cola and Pepsi: A Comparative Analysis in the Indian Market. *International Journal of Conceptions on Management and Social Sciences* 2 (2): 2357–2787.

Hsieh, T. 2010. *Delivering Happiness: A Path to Profits, Passion, and Purpose*. New York: Grand Central Publishing.

Okazaki, S. 2006. Excitement or Sophistication? A Preliminary Exploration of Online Brand Personality. *International Marketing Review* 23 (3): 279–303.

Chapter 11

Creative Strategy

Learning Objectives

This chapter is intended to help you:

- Understand the role of a creative strategy for a brand
- Understand the purpose and outcomes of a creative brief
- Examine the elements of a creative brief
- Understand how to deal with different messages under the same strategy

What Is Creative Strategy and the Creative Brief?

The creative strategy is very similar to a brand message strategy and a communication strategy in that it reflects specific objectives of the brand and points the way that the objectives can be achieved. The key difference with a creative strategy is that the primary audience for the strategy is people who are going to be developing the creative work: the advertisements, the public relations efforts, the website and the social media messages: anything that is associated with a specific goal of the brand. A creative strategy presents the strategic choices that were agreed upon by the client and its agents to achieve the goal, and inspires the people creating messages to craft communications that will resonate with the target. Advertising account planner Jon Steel (1998) described the creative brief as the bridge between strategic thinking and advertising. Lisa Fortini-Campbell (2001) has described the creative brief as the document that "introduces the creative department to the person they'll be talking to." In that way, the creative brief is "an advertisement to influence the creative team" (Steel, 1998, p. 149).

The creative strategy is provided to the creative team developing messages via a mechanism called the creative brief, although some people refer to this as the creative platform or simply the creative strategy. However, the term "brief" is important. The word brief means concise and free of superfluous detail. And that is what a good creative brief is: a distillation of all your research into clients' products, services, and ideas, and the reactions of consumers and other stakeholders into insights that will inspire great work from others.

The Role of the Creative Brief

The creative brief is a communications tool that starts a dialogue among members of the brand team. Many people wonder, then, why a brief is put into writing.

- The brief sets the boundaries within which the advertising will be developed. It serves several other purposes and thus documents the decisions and processes that are to be followed as the work is developed.
- Creative briefs track how advertising messages are developed over time. They provide a history and help agencies and clients recognize what worked and what didn't.
- Creative briefs are a point of agreement among everyone involved in the advertising at both the agency and client level. Clients will be asked to approve the creative brief, thereby indicating their agreement to the strategic direction of the creative brief. This can be especially beneficial if client personnel changes during the course of the campaign development. The client-approved creative brief is in essence a contract that will provide clients an indication of what the advertising will communicate, and it may mitigate potential conflicts during a personnel change.
- Creative briefs are a reference point for creative teams, in that they can continuously refer to the creative brief to keep them on track as they develop the advertising.
- Creative briefs allow the agency and client account teams to develop a somewhat objective evaluation of the advertising, because the communication achieved by the advertising can be compared to the communication goals set out in the creative brief.

Creative briefs were once under the purview of the advertising agency and were used only to develop advertising executions. Today, creative briefs are used in a variety of marketing situations. These include: advertising, web design, public relations activities such as news releases and events, social media engagements, logo development, and for sponsorships. Having one creative brief to build projects from will mean that the branding stays clear, consistent, and constant, and that all pieces of the communications effort work together.

The Basics of the Creative Brief

Many agencies have their own formats and/or formulas for what goes into a creative brief, as you will notice in the examples provided in this chapter. While the actual formats and terminology may be different, creative briefs tend to all encompass a similar set of information.

Objective or Statement of Purpose

In this first section, the creative brief address questions such as: Why are we advertising? What is the problem that advertising can solve? How will the client benefit? How will consumers benefit?

Advertising can play several roles in solving a problem:

1) It can *generate awareness* of a product or service that a consumer has never heard about, or awareness of new aspects of the product or service that can solve a problem.
2) It can *inform and educate consumers* about how a product or service can specifically solve their problem.
3) It can *change consumer attitudes or perceptions* about a product.
4) It can *create an identity* associating a product with a person.
5) It can *gain trial* or influence repurchase of a brand.

The objective will be closely related to the marketing goals established by the client in the marketing plan. If there are several levels of marketing goals, it is necessary to prioritize them carefully and assess which are best addressed through advertising. Addressing too many messages will dilute the impact of the message and will make messages confusing. Relating the communication objective to the marketing objective provides the ability to measure the success of the campaign once it is completed. In our mythical cell service provider AllCell, for example, we identified several communications objectives (see Table 11.1):

Table 11.1
AllCell Communication Objectives

Brand Objective	Communication Objective
To increase coverage to 95% of the United States	Create awareness of our coverage strength relative to competitors among 85% of customers over the next six months
To provide optimal customer service to all clients	Create knowledge of awards won in customer service area among all consumers over the next year
To increase customer retention by 10% by offering a loyalty program	Create desire to continue with the service among 30% of consumers
	Increase engagement and interactions on key social media channels with 25% more interactions per week

Tied into the objective might be some additional background about the brand or a specific articulation of the problem that must be solved. On some briefs, this problem is articulated in the form of the "consumer's current response," that is, what the consumer is likely to say today when asked about the client. Often, these responses are direct quotes gathered from qualitative research, and strongly suggest what issues need to be overcome.

When examining what was happening in the mobile landscape, we saw that about 10 percent of all cell phone users switch their service in an average year. For our client, though, we noticed that about 15 percent of our users left us in an average year. Therefore, we chose to focus on the customer retention objective and the communication objective to increase desire among the service. This would address a key business objective. The current response for this client might be "All cell phone services are alike—why don't I just look for the cheapest?" or "There's no good reason to stick with my current provider."

Competition

Both short-term and long-term competitors should be identified. For our cell phone service, for example, short-term competition might be all cell phone service providers, longer-term competition might include cable service phone providers, landlines, and any emerging technologies that may offer a similar service.

In examining cell phone competitors, we noted that most companies focus on either price or coverage strength. Both of these strategies are highly short term, as companies are constantly creating new promotions to entice switching and adding new geographic coverage (and in reality, we are not far from the day when everyone in the United States has coverage everywhere). While our client can compete on price, if the client has learned that consumers are (not surprisingly) highly confused by all the plans, fees, and charges that are encountered with their cell phones, particularly when it comes to switching. So the idea to focus on something other than this can help the brand stand out from others, especially if it makes low cost a support point to its primary message and finds ways to provide pricing information simply, via other messages.

Target Audience

The creative brief should present the strategy from the consumer's point of view, and the target audience section of the creative brief presents the target from numerous perspectives, such as demographically, psychographically, and in terms of product/service usage and behavior. The target audience description should be both descriptive and emotional, identifying aspects of the group that bind consumers together. This can be done by providing insights into how consumers think and feel.

Here are three potential target audiences for our campaign:

1) Cell phone users aged 18–34, particularly Hispanics and African Americans, who are considering switching their cell phone service. One leading research firm reports that this group is most likely to switch in a given year.

2) Cell phone users aged 18–34, particularly Hispanics and African Americans who use their phones as a way to stay connected to their family members, both in town and far away, and to their networks of friends. This is also a generation of cord-cutters—most of them do not have landlines at home so their cell phone is their primary connection method.
3) Cell phone users aged 18-34, particularly Hispanics and African Americans whose phones are physically connected to their hands; they consider themselves opinion leaders in their groups and rely on their phones to maintain their connections to the world to keep then as leaders in their groups.

After reading the first example, do you have an image in your mind of the consumer? The first example provides standard demographic information that is somewhat vague. The second example provides quite a bit of information, but no real inspiration: the description is likely to fit virtually every 18–34 year old in the United States. The third example creates a much more vivid picture in the mind of everyone reading the creative brief. It describes what is unique and different about the people who are part of a larger target audience; it is possible to picture an individual fitting into this group in your mind. Exhibit 11.1 provides another example of the way to describe a target.

Big Idea

This is sometimes termed the "key insight," "the single most compelling thought," or "key promise"; it is what you hope consumers will take away from the advertising message. The insight will pull together all the research and show how it fits into the bigger context of the advertising message. The techniques described earlier in this book should help you to discover the key consumer insights that will motivate consumers to purchase your brand.

When thinking about the Big Idea, sometimes it is best to think about the idea as a question. We presented some options for a big idea for All-Cell based on Maslow's Hierarchy, repeated in Table 11.2. We've added a way to think about the strength as a question in order to create a Big Idea.

Exhibit 11.1: Creative Brief

Problem: Many people switch cell phone services every year.

Objective: Create the desire to continue with the service among 30 percent of consumers.

Target Audience: Cell phone users 18–34 particularly Hispanics and African Americans whose phones are physically connected to their hands; they consider themselves opinion leaders in their groups and rely on their phones to maintain their connections to the world to keep them as leaders in their groups.

Current Response: All cell phone services are alike; I might as well look for the cheapest one.

Single Most important thought: "With AllCell, there's no need to be constantly checking out the competition, so you will always be connected."

Desired Response, Current Customers: "My service has everything I need, so no need to switch."
Desired Response, Potential customers: "I want to always be connected . . . I will look into that service."

Tone: Cheerful and reliable

Mandatory Inclusions: All messages should include AllCell's web address (allcellmobile.com) and Twitter handle (@allcellmobile).

As a next step, we can start to think about the types of demonstrations and metaphors that might work for these ideas (as seen in Table 11.3).

For the one big idea for the AllCell campaign, we are going to select "always be connected." Our message in the creative brief will be phrased as follows:

> "With AllCell we are constantly looking at what our competitors are doing so you don't have to. We take the responsibility so you will always be connected."

Table 11.2
Possible Key Strategic Ideas for AllCell

	Strength	Question	Connection
Physiological	Only the strong survive	How do we show the strength of something invisible (a phone service)	There's someone there for you
Safety	Never lose a call	How do we show the USP of low dropped call rates?	Always be connected
Belonging	Be part of the group that is #1	How do we show who the group is?	Never be disconnected
Esteem	People want to be part of your group	How do we demonstrate the benefit of being in a group?	We are always there for you
Self-actualization	Only the strong survive	How do we show strength in a unique way?	I am always there

Table 11.3
Demonstrations and Metaphors for All Cell

Strength	Connection	Vivid demonstration	Vivid metaphor
Only the strong survive	There's someone there for you.	Demonstrate the people involved in the company	Associate with someone aspirational or who inspires confidence
Never lose a call	Always be connected	Compare to others	Associate with an authority figure
Be part of the group that is #1	Never be disconnected	Define the group	Associate with people like people in the target
People want to be part of your group	We are always there for you.	Define the group	Demonstrate the target's popularity
Only the strong survive	I am always there.	Claim it first	Associate with a strong individual

Support

The support points are the reasons why the big idea is valid and why the target will believe the message focus. Support points can include both product attributes and consumer attitudes.

For the All Cell message, our support points will include:

- Competitive rates every day
- Strongest coverage in the United States
- Award-winning team of customer service professionals to help you when you need it
- Use your time to connect with friends and family and not negotiate with other companies

Desired Response

Creative briefs can also include a "desired response" or what we expect the members of the target audience to say after they have engaged with our campaign. This response should be, of course, significantly different than the current response. For our cell phone provider, a desired response would be:

> "I trust that my service has everything I need, so no need to switch."
> or
> "I want to always be connected . . . I will look in to that service."

Mandatory Inclusions

Often, a message must include some specific information for legal reasons. For example, advertising for many types of bank products must by law include specific financial disclosure information. The beer beverage industry has a guideline that adults not be shown actually drinking beer in commercials. Other guidelines might be client directed, such as the amount of time the brand logo has to be shown at the end of a television commercial, or what web address should be included.

Style or Tone

Remember the idea of a brand personality that we discussed in Chapter 10? This should be introduced again in the style or tone section of the brief. The style or tone should be directional in nature and should, again, broadly define boundaries for the people creating the advertisements.

The Language of the Creative Brief

The written creative brief should be both directional and inspirational. It is directional in that it should let the creative team know what is required of the advertising, in terms of advertising goals as well as specific information that must be included. This will be enhanced if the creative brief is sharply focused and neither verbose nor ambiguous.

The creative brief should be inspirational in that it encourages the creative team to strive to create the best advertising possible. To be inspirational, the creative brief should be imaginative, stimulating, and involving. To use an artistic metaphor, the creative brief should be the palette of paints presented to the artist (the creative team) for the creation of a masterpiece. Take for example, two different ways to describe consumer insights regarding our cell phone client:

1) "You don't need to switch services, since AllCell has strong coverage, great customer service, and competitive rates."
2) "With AllCell, there's no need to be constantly checking out the competition, so you will always be connected."

The first example is unexciting. It provides direction but does not necessarily inspire the creative team, and it is also focused on the brand, not the consumer. The second example presents a more vivid description of the insight, is focused on the consumer and not the brand, and can help the creative team focus their energy into the optimal message for the advertisement. Try to write as visually as you can; see if your words sound like words consumers in your target would say or would react to.

The important thing to think about is emotion: your Big Idea will want to hit an emotion that is relevant to the audience AND to the brand. Emotions are either positive or negative: you will want to either accentuate a positive emotion or replace a negative emotion.

Some positive emotions a brand can highlight include:

- Enjoyment: delight, price, and satisfaction
- Love: friendliness, trust, and adoration
- Surprise: wonder or amazement

Some negative emotions a brand can replace include:

- Surprise, shock, or astonishment
- Disgust, contempt, or revulsion
- Shame, guilt, or regret
- Anger, outrage, or resentment
- Sadness, grief, or loneliness
- Fear, anxiety, or nervousness

Assessing the Creative Brief

Once the creative brief is drafted but before it is presented to the creative team, the planner should check it over, asking him- or herself the following questions.

➤ Is the Creative Brief Consistent?

We use the word consistent throughout this book, and the creative brief is no exception. The elements of the creative brief should work back clearly to the business and marketing objectives, and the elements of the creative brief should fit together logically in that each piece of information builds upon the information previously provided. The creative brief should be committed to a point of view.

➤ Is the Creative Brief Believable and Supportable?

Not only must the creative brief be logical and insightful, it must also be believable. That will help ensure that the team's ultimate creative approach is inherently right for the target audience. A great way to do this is to provide backup research to support every claim presented in the brief.

➤ Is the Creative Brief Clear and Simple?

The creative brief should be written in language that the consumer would use, and as a result will be clear to anyone reading it. To make sure it is simple, strive to fit the creative brief onto a single page, which will make sure only the most important insights are presented. Although this may seem like an arbitrary cut-off point for such an important document, Roman and Maas (1992) argue that if you can't fit the information onto one page, the chances of getting it all into a 30-second commercial are slight. For longer form messages, longer briefs may be used.

➤ Is This a Good Introduction of the Consumer to the Team?

Will people be able to visualize the consumer—to see him or her during her daily activities—to hear the sound of his or her voice? If so, then the brief is a good one.

How would the All Cell brief look in final form? Exhibit 11.1 shows this.

Using the Creative Brief Across Multiple Messages

As we mentioned at the beginning of the chapter, a creative brief can be the starting point for a number of different types of communications. Some of the elements such as the problem target audience, the current and desired responses, the single most important thought, and the tone will be consistent. However, the objective is likely to change, as well as the mandatory requirements.

Let's consider AllCell and how the objectives might change given the type of communication effort:

- Advertising objective: Create the desire to continue with the service among 30 percent of consumers
- Public relations objective: Create 1,000,000 impressions through 50 placements in national print and broadcast outlets focusing on exceptional customer service
- Website objective: Create an online experience where customers can find the information they seek within 15 seconds of arriving at the site

- Social media objective: Earn 1,000 new followers each month and create 10 positive consumer mentions on social media each week

For executions in different channels, the mandatories should include some of the creative work developed and used in the other executions. A logo, for example, should be consistent across work, but perhaps the color palette of the logo can change depending on the channel if that makes sense for the brand. The specific size and placement of the logo might also be important to be considered. If advertising messages use a spokesperson, the mandatories should indicate if this spokesperson should be included in other executions, such as the brand's social media presence and website.

Summary

The creative strategy is documented through the creative brief. The creative brief is an important tool that provides direction to the creative teams developing messages for the brand. Elements of the creative brief are generally consistent although they may be labeled differently at different agencies.

Review questions

1. Who is involved in the creation of the creative brief?
2. Who is the audience for the creative brief?
3. What is the difference between the "current response" and the "desired response"?
4. Where does information for the creative brief come from?

Discussion Questions

1. Why is it important to provide a vivid description of the target audience?
2. Is the AllCell brief (Exhibit 11.1) consistent, believable, supportable, clear, and simple? Why or why not? How could it be improved?
3. Do you agree with the creative brief for AllCell? If you changed one element, would other elements change?

4. Bell Bicycle Helmets is targeting mothers with kids between the ages of 6 and 15 to address a key problem: Kids don't like to wear helmets and often parents don't fight them about it because they are just riding around the neighborhood. Most parents also think helmets are all alike, aren't aware that Bell helmets are the safest helmets on the market (Bell pioneered the concept of safety); they sell more helmets than anyone else, and are the choice of professionals. Identify a message associated with each of these advertising roles:
   - o generate awareness
   - o inform and educate
   - o change consumer attitudes or perceptions
   - o create an identity
   - o gain trial
5. Select one message and show examples of how you can accentuate a positive emotion or replace a negative emotion in that message.

Additional Resources

Fortini-Campbell, L. 2001. *Hitting the Sweet Spot: How Consumer Insights Can Inspire Better Marketing and Advertising*. Chicago: Copy Workshop.

Mondroski, M. M., L. N. Reid, and J. T. Russell. 1983. Agency Creative Decision Making: A Decision Systems Analysis. *Journal of Current Issues and Research in Advertising* 23: 57–69.

Philips, P. L. 2004. *Creating the Perfect Design Brief: How to Manage Design for Strategic Advantage*. London: Allworth Press.

Roman, K., and J. Maas. 1992. *The New How to Advertise*. New York: St. Martin's.

Steel, J. 1998. *Truth, Lies and Advertising: The Art of Account Planning*. New York: John Wiley & Sons.

Chapter 12

Media Strategy

Learning Objectives

This chapter is intended to help you:

- Understand the unique aspects of media strategy and what it is intended to achieve
- Recognize the difference between media objectives and other types of objectives, such as marketing and communication objectives
- Distinguish between a brand target, a media planning target, and a media measurement target
- Understand different media strategies

Today's Media Landscape

The media landscape today is a rich combination of a variety of channels to deliver the message. One way to think about the variety of messages is to think about them in terms of owned, earned, and paid media.

Owned media are all the channels that a brand controls, including (but not limited to) the brand's website, mobile site, blog, Twitter and Facebook accounts. Owned media work well for creating long-term relationships with existing customers, which should lead to earned media. The benefits to the brand are the ability to have complete control over the message, and the cost efficiencies from the ownership. On the downside, though, there are no guarantees that people will become regular visitors to your owned media sites. At the same time, some consumers are naturally distrustful of corporate messages.

Earned media are mentions by consumers themselves, also known as word-of-mouth (or electronic word-of-mouth in the digital sphere), "buzz," or messages that go viral. For earned media to work, brands must provide content that consumers can respond to and then listen and respond to what they see. Earned media is highly credible and influential, but brands give up a high level of control over the message. Some brands are so afraid of negative earned media that they avoid using it altogether.

Paid media are media channels that brands pay to leverage: traditional advertising, paid search on sites like Google, and sponsorships. These messages can provide content for owned media as well as stimulate earned media. Brands have a good level of control over most aspects of paid media, but consumers also have control in that they can choose to pay attention to such messages or not.

Media strategy is the strategy surrounding HOW messages will be delivered to target audiences. It develops the framework for assessing which media will be used to reach the specific audiences for specific messages. Media strategies are often developed by the media department of the advertising agency.

Like the other strategies described in this book, media strategies contain several areas including:

- Media objectives
- Strategies to accomplish objectives
- Target audience strategies
- Media mix strategies
- Scheduling strategies
- Geographic strategies

Setting Media Objectives

Media objectives come directly from both the marketing and the communication objectives. As you have come to learn from this book, the marketing objectives themselves stem from the brand's overall business goals. Because both the business and the marketing objectives are used in so many additional strategic areas, it is important to reiterate that these objectives must be smart, measurable, attainable, realistic, and trackable, and the media objectives must be as well.

Sometimes it is helpful to take a step back at this point and ask a question: What is one thing that the brand would like to accomplish this year? Some people may say "to have our core buyer buy more. If every core buyer just made one additional purchase, we would achieve our sales goals." Then you can ask about a second thing, and a third thing, if you'd like. This helps to prioritize both the target audience and specific aspects of the media plan.

The media objectives should then connect directly to these business goals. For example, if the marketing plan calls for trial of a new product, several media objectives might be included such as:

- Generate awareness among 85 percent of the target audience during the first two months of the product's introduction
- Drive 25,000 downloads of a $1 off digital coupon from our website during the second two months of the product's introduction
- Stimulate positive word-of-mouth during the first six months of the introduction

These objectives clearly indicate that paid media (awareness advertising, coupon), owned media (website) and earned media (word-of-mouth) will all contribute to meeting the goals and are necessary for the introduction of this new product. These objectives are all quantifiable objectives that support the larger goal and will direct the development of the strategies that follow. Once the media plan moves to the tactical stage, it will be clear how individual tactics connect with the objectives.

Some media people may be very concerned about these quantifiable objectives, particularly the ones about downloads. This concern comes from peoples' desires to want to succeed and not fail (by not meeting an objective). However, not having a quantifiable media objective makes optimizing the media plan very difficult, particularly because it makes it almost impossible to pivot and try something new if goals are not met (and with a goal of 25,000 downloads during a two month period, you can generally tell within the first two weeks whether the goal will be met based on online metrics that are easily available). Hoping for the best (with an ambiguous goal) no longer cuts it in the media world.

Sometimes media objectives contain goals regarding reach and frequency. *Reach* is the number or percent of different homes or persons exposed at least once to an advertising schedule over a specific period of time. Reach, then, excludes duplication. *Frequency* is the number of times that the average household or person is exposed to the schedule among those persons reached in the specific period of time. Because it is an average frequency, dispersion of frequency of exposure will differ between specific schedules and daypart mixes. Such an objective would be framed as follows:

- ➤ Develop 90 percent reach of the target audience with each target audience member exposed an average of five times over a six-week period.

Other objectives may include a recency goal, which is how close to the actual purchase the target audience member will be exposed to a message.

- ➤ Reach 70 percent of the target audience at least twice in the two days prior to the start of the sale on Friday.

How do you know if your media objective is a good one? Here's a simple test—if some other media people look at the objective and understand what needs to be done and how it can be measured, then the objective is a good one.

Deciding Media Strategies

The media strategy describes how the objective will be accomplished and, like the objective, it needs to be clear and concise. You should be able to easily answer the question, "How will you accomplish the objective?" While related, the objective and the strategy are two distinct elements. The objective describes the desired outcomes that will be accomplished; the strategy describes the activities to achieve the outcomes.

- Objective: Generate awareness among 85 percent of the target audience during the first two months of the product's introduction
    - ➤ Strategy: utilize broad reach media to stimulate awareness
- Objective: Drive 25,000 downloads of a $1 off digital coupon from our website during the second two months of the product's introduction

  - Strategy: utilize digital channels to direct consumers to website
  - Strategy: highlight coupon on website during the promotional period
- Objective: Stimulate positive word-of-mouth during the first six months of the introduction
  - Strategy: encourage purchase and reviews via social media sites

When crafting strategies, there is a great temptation to include tactics or the specific media vehicles that you think should be used for the strategy. Strategies are big ideas, while tactics are concrete specific actions that will be taken. There can be many different tactics that can be related to a strategy, although there are generally only a few strategies that will be related to an objective. Here's an example:

- Objective: Generate awareness among 85 percent of the target audience during the first two months of the product's introduction
  - Strategy: utilize broad reach media to stimulate awareness
    - Tactic: focus on prime-time television to build awareness among the target
    - Tactic: focus on sports programming to build awareness among the target

It is important to avoid writing tactics in place of strategies. It's also important to note that your strategy may still work to meet your objective even when one or all of your tactics aren't working. In the example above, it wouldn't be possible to generate high levels of awareness with media vehicles that are more frequency-oriented, like radio or outdoor. Data and research will usually be needed to support a strategy: for example, why are reach vehicles better for generating the desired levels of awareness? You might wish to provide a summary of the awareness-building capabilities of major media.

Selecting the Target Audience

We have discussed target audiences throughout this book. It is important to note, though, the media planning targets may not be as well-defined as the brand planning target, merely for lack of available data at the measurement stage. Here is an example based on our fictional cell phone company AllCell:

- Brand Planning Target: Cell phone users aged 18–34 particularly Hispanics and African Americans whose phones are physically connected to their hands; they consider themselves opinion leaders in their groups and rely on their phones to maintain their connections to the world in order to keep then as leaders in their groups.
- Media planning Target: Cell phone users aged 18–34, particularly Hispanics and African Americans, particularly based on cord-cutters and what we know about them and their media habits.
- Media Measurement Target—Simple demographics like:
    - Primary: Hispanic and African American Adults aged 18–34
    - Secondary: Caucasians and Asians aged 18–34

Note that the media planning target is often defined in terms of psychographics and the media measurement target audience is often defined in terms of demographics. The term "psychographics" refers to consumers' personality traits (serious, funny, conservative), beliefs and attitudes about social issues (opinions about abortion, environment, globalization), personal interests (music, sports, movie going), and shopping orientations (recreational shoppers, price-sensitive shoppers, convenience shoppers).

Syndicated research services such as Simmons Market Research Bureau (SMRB or Simmons) and Mediamark Research & Intelligence (MRI) provide national data on a number of demographics of U.S. consumers, including gender, age, education, household income, marital status, employment status, type of residence, and number of children in the household. Some advertisers believe that demographic definitions of a target audience are too ambiguous, because individual consumers that fit such definitions can be quite different in terms of their brand preference and purchase behavior. These are seen in the media planning target.

Media Mix Strategy

Which mix of media should the brand use? The media mix is the combination of all the various communication channels the brand could utilize to meet its marketing objectives. When making media mix decisions, all the opportunities that consumers have for contact with the brand should be considered, including those in the digital sphere and the promotion sphere.

The media mix is a two-step process first involving determining the correct mix of paid, earned, and owned media. The second part of the process is determining the correct mix of paid media, as most plans will include some (if not all) paid media.

Both of these steps in the process begin with the media objective. Earlier in the chapter we presented this objective: Generate awareness among 85 percent of the target audience during the first two months of the product's introduction.

One media mix strategy would be to use only paid media for this campaign. The rationale for this would be that it is relatively straightforward to assess whether the goal has been met; we could argue that it takes four exposures for someone to be aware of the new product, so we could attempt to reach 85 percent of the target audience at least four times during the first two months of the campaign. We would have control over when the messages would be seen and be able to directly measure the actual reach and frequency. Consumer research could occur after the two month period to measure actual awareness.

The downside to the paid-only strategy is the cost. Let's say it costs, on average, $50 per thousand to reach adults during prime time. There are about 130 million adults aged 18–49 in the United States— to reach 85 percent would cost about $5.5 million (130,000 × .85 × 50).

In general, earned and owned media is quite a bit less expensive, so we could add them to the mix strategically for this new product introduction. Let's say we relied on paid media to reach a bit less than 50 percent of the target audience—that would cut the paid budget in half. We could then feature the new product significantly on owned media (the brand website) and create a social media plan to direct online followers to the website; we could plan to reach about 20 percent of the target audience in this manner. The brand could hire a public relations firm to create press releases and videos to promote the new product in the media; such an effort might cost about $100,000 to reach about 20 percent of the target audience. Specific costs will vary, of course, based on how the brand is staffed, but adding earned and owned media would present the brand in ways that fit into people's lives, would generate some comments and shares, and would work to build awareness. The brand has less control, but with proper monitoring of the response and pivoting with channels as necessary, the new product launch could be very successful.

Taco Bell is one brand that does this well. When it launched Cool Ranch Tacos, social media was used to leak the location of a flower shop in Manhattan that was giving out the product for free. The catch: people needed a "secret password" available only on social media. The launch was supported with a press release and national media coverage of the event, and followed with a Super Bowl ad.

The second part of the media mix includes the evaluation of paid media in two areas: effectiveness and efficiency. Effectiveness is assessed by the usage of the medium by all members of the target audience. Taco Bell, for example, selected the Super Bowl as a channel since it receives huge viewership and people tend to pay attention to the commercials more than during other programs.

For our cell phone provider target, Hispanic and African American men aged 18–34 tend to use mobile media more than other target audiences and for all types of activities including reading news, playing games, listening to music, and using coupons.

Efficiency is measured in the cost to reach a thousand members of the audience using the vehicle. While the cost per thousand of a television advertisement for this target is around $50; for some mobile media, the cost per thousand is less than $3. This makes mobile an efficient vehicle for the cell phone provider, where the Super Bowl might be out of their range.

However, we are not likely to recommend a mix of only mobile messages. There is often quite a bit of clutter in the mobile landscape and we might be able to use some specific targeting on television media—such as extreme sports programs and shows on MTV—to reach this audience as well.

Scheduling Strategy

The media strategy may also propose a scheduling pattern to show when the media messages will be delivered during the course of a campaign or a year. There are three general strategies that are used in scheduling:

- Continuous: scheduling a consistent and sustainable level of media presence/support during the entire campaign period
- Flighting: scheduling concentrated media support/presence during specific times of the year (known as a peak) with hiatus periods in between the peaks
- Pulsing: scheduling a low level of consistent support with occasional peaks during the campaign period

Geography

In addition to allocating advertising by media category, media planners must allocate advertising by geography. In general, a company that sells nationally can take one of three approaches to geographic spending allocation:

1) a *national approach* (advertise in all markets),
2) a *spot approach* (advertise only in selected markets), or
3) a *combined* national plus spot approach (advertise in all markets with additional spending in selected markets).

Media planners will choose a national approach if sales are relatively uniform across the country. A national approach will reach a national customer base with a national advertising program. This could be used for our fictional client if switchers live all across the country (which they probably do). However, if research showed that potential switchers tend to live mostly in the Northeast, we could use a spot approach more efficiently. If there were several smaller geographic areas where we found switchers at a bit more of a concentration, we would use a combined approach.

Displaying the Strategy via Flow Chart

The media flowchart provides a visual summary of when different strategic elements will occur. The effectiveness of a media campaign largely depends on timing. Your media should be released when the need for it is greatest. For example, for a new product introduction, high levels of media will be needed to quickly build awareness. Then, a digital program would kick in to direct people to the downloadable coupon.

Measurement

The measurement of the actual delivery (and hence the effectiveness) of the actual media schedule is generally conducted by the advertising agency or the media-buying service using published ratings. Additionally, tracking of increases in awareness can be done through surveys and digital metrics. Couponing strategies can be assessed by examining the number of different coupons redeemed in store. For television and radio ratings, the post-analysis compares on a program-by-program basis the estimated delivery of a spot (during the planning stage) compared to the actual delivery of the spot (after it airs). Other *feedback devices* such as reply cards, toll-free numbers, coupons and web addresses can be provided in ads so that tallies of the responses or redemptions can be made to estimate the impact of advertising media

Finally, marketers can use observation techniques to better understand audience reactions, identify point-of-purchase effectiveness, and assess marketing events. For example, researchers can be stationed in grocery stores to observe how consumers react to in-store advertising or how they select an advertised brand in comparison with other brands. Researchers can join shoppers on trips to the mall. Online observation can also happen by receiving permission to track an individual's activities over a specific period of time. The advantage of observation is that it provides rich, detailed data on how consumers behave in real situations in response to the marketing communication. The downside is that direct observation is more costly to conduct and tabulate.

Summary

The media strategy provides specific information on how the brand's objectives will be met. Media objectives derive from communication objectives and media strategies derive from the media objectives. The media strategy also includes strategies regarding the target audience, the media mix, scheduling, and geography.

Review Questions

1. What are the differences between paid, earned, and owned media? How do these work together in a strategy?
2. What are the differences between a media objective and a media strategy?
3. What is the difference between a media strategy and a media tactic?
4. What are the differences between a brand planning target, a media planning target, and a media measurement target? Why can't these targets all be the same?
5. What are three types of scheduling patterns? Give an example of why a brand may use one of these.

Discussion Questions

1. If a brand is available nationally, should it always use a national media plan? Explain your answer.
2. Have you ever seen an ad for a product or service that is not in your geographic area? Why did you see it? What are the pros and cons for this type of activity for the brand?
3. Can a media channel be efficient and not effective? Effective and not efficient? Talk about situations when this might happen.

Additional Resources

Katz, Helen. 2013. *The Media Handbook: A Complete Guide to Advertising Media Selection, Planning, Research, and Buying*. 5th ed. New York: Routledge.

Kelley, L., K. Sheehan, and D. Jugenheimer. 2014. *Advertising Media Planning: A Brand Management Approach*. 4th ed. New York: Routledge.

Chapter 13

Brand Association Strategy

Learning Objectives

This chapter is intended to help you:

- Understand the benefits and challenges of developing partnerships with other brands
- Understand the benefits and challenges of developing partnerships with causes and other charitable entities
- Develop best practices for brand partnership strategies

Introduction

Have you ever bought coffee at a Starbucks outlet in a Barnes & Noble bookstore? Or bought a package of M&Ms that were filled with Peter Pan peanut butter? Perhaps your Subaru Forrester is a customized "L. L. Bean" SUV? Have you shopped at Target for an Orla Kiely wallet or at H&M for an Alexander Wang scarf? Perhaps you wash your clothes with Tide that contains Febreze or wash your dishes with Dawn that contains Cascade (products that are called "co-branded")? As you can see, brand partnerships are seen everywhere we go, for all types of products. We also see brands partnering with nonprofit organizations: IKEA with Save the Children; UNICEF and Gillette with Movember (a charity to raise funds for testicular and prostate cancer); and a plethora of companies including American Airlines, Ford Motors, Zipcar, and the Dallas Cowboys partner with the Susan G. Komen foundation.

The phenomenon of multiple brands participating in a single message strategy is becoming more prevalent in society today. Partnerships create synergies for all partners involved but it is important to note that for a partnership to work, there must be both a clear strategy and clear benefits for all partners. This chapter will first discuss strategies for a brand to partner with another brand, and then strategies for a brand to partner with a nonprofit or charity.

Strategic Connections and Trade-offs

Any type of brand association is going to involve some investment of resources—time, money, talent—in the association. These are resources that are going to go away from the "solo" brand message. Some key things to remember about this trade-off:

- Be sure the progress toward the brand's own goals are on track; anticipate how such goals might need to be revised given the redirection of resources to a brand association.
- Investigate changes to existing tactics that might result in some cost savings in order to fund brand associations as discussed in the previous chapter. Again, revisit these tactics in light of progress toward brand goals.
- Identify key people available to participate in brand association activities, and make identify-specific challenges to their current responsibilities that should be addressed prior to the association.
- Identify the specific weakness that a brand partnership will address for your brand, and evaluate the different types of associations based on that specific weakness. Not every option will be best for every brand, and not every brand will have the resources available to participate in every opportunity. Prioritizing what your brand needs will help guide these decisions.

Brand Associations with a Specific Branded Offering

One of the most straightforward ways to make a brand association is by partnering with an existing offering such as a branded certification or seal of approval. Examples of this are:

- The Good Housekeeping Seal of Approval: Brands submit products for testing to the Good Housekeeping labs, where effectiveness and marketing claims are studied. Consumers who purchase products with the seal are given a two-year limited warranty against product defects. Thousands of products carry the seal. Products must have the seal to run in the magazine, and products obtaining the seal must run ads in the magazine. Certification can take up to two months.

- Google Partners is a certification that is given to agencies and other advertisers who pass an exam. "To be a Google certified partner, an agency must have at least two Adwords Certified individuals, follow all 'Best Practices' from Google, and must have managed a $10,000 spend in at least 60 of the last 90 days, and been active in the last 90 days" (Wikipedia 2016).
- Fairtrade International is a certification program of companies that meet the Fairtrade standards which cover how brands work with different producers and how much is paid for raw materials. Certification, through FLO-Cert, can cost several thousands of dollars and must be renewed annually.
- Whole Foods has an Eco-seal rating system for cleaning products sold in its stores. Every product is rated based on how it meets third party verification standards and whether it has been tested on animals and contains a variety of chemical ingredients.

The benefits of these types of certifications are:

- Such established associations are highly visible
- These are also seen as highly credible in the minds of consumers
- There are clear guidelines on what a brand needs to do in order to participate in the association
- They generally come with a low cost and can be relatively quick to obtain

Some of the downsides are:

- Other competitors in the category may have the association, so this may not be a way to establish a clear point of difference from competitors

- If another brand with the certification is found to be faulty, it may invalidate the certification and as a result any brand equity in the certification
- Costs of certification may be more than any cost benefit from certification

Brand Associations with Another Brand

As we mentioned at the beginning, a brand association is an association between two (or more) brands. This association often happens in persuasive messages but can also happen in the digital sphere, at the store level, and at events.

Brand associations have numerous benefits:

- Associations can be cost-efficient as two (or more) brands share in the costs of a single message program.
- Associations can raise awareness and value of both brands: the idea that one can get a Starbucks' coffee at a Barnes & Noble may cause people to decide to shop at that store rather than at an alternative or online. While Barnes & Noble could have opened their own coffee shops, they recognized the increase in their brand value would be stronger with the Starbucks connection. Starbucks could quickly build their reach and coverage.
- Associations can change perceptions of brands—Target's and H&M's partnerships with high-end designers add a sense of glamour and value to these low-end retailers. The designers get mass-market exposure which can eventually assist them in getting future licensing contracts.
- Associations can increase sales of both products as consumers who have an affinity for one brand may purchase the partner brand because of that affinity.
- Associations can increase customer and brand loyalty since such partnerships give consumers a new reason to purchase the brands.
- Associations can attract media coverage, particularly if the partnership is innovative and unexpected. An innovative partnership can make brands appear more contemporary,

distinctive, interesting, and noteworthy. The Ace Hotel in New York City, for example, partners with different artists who provide artwork for their hotel rooms. The artwork is also available for sale. The hotel becomes essentially a giant art gallery, and this association gets quite a bit of press coverage.

These associations can have some downsides, in terms of:

- Minimal control over activities of the other brand outside of the partnership
- Perceptions of inequality between each brand
- Extensive resources (time and money) are generally needed.

Developing a Brand Association Strategy

It is essential that a strategic partnership present a win-win situation for all brands that are part of the partnership. Without this goal, there is the possibility that one brand will not pull their weight or participate as fully as they should to make the association a success. Here are some key steps.

1) **Review your own brand objectives** and be clear on how a partnership will help you meet them. A brand association strategy must bring benefits to your brand that builds into your business strategy. Part of this is making sure not only the products or services are compatible, but also that the target audiences are compatible.
2) **Review your key strategic idea** when identifying possible partners for a brand association. Brand partners should have brands that present complimentary value perceptions among consumers. For example, Subaru is seen as a brand for active people who enjoy the outdoors, as is L. L. Bean. M&Ms and Peter Pan are both brands that appeal to children as well to adults looking for a treat. Partners should be strong brands in their own right, with broad or growing awareness. Brands' meaningful emotional connections with customers is also important.

At the same time, brand teams must be able to work together to execute the plan, must agree on an appropriate target audience, and must commit budgets that address each brand's expected gains. For example, it is likely that M&Ms and Peter Pan contributed equal amounts for their partnership budget as both products are relatively low-priced and have a similar target audience.

3) **Conduct due diligence**—when considering possible partners, look to see whether the brand has previously worked in a partnership. If so, contact the partner brand team to find out about outcomes and what the experiences were with the partner. What is the overall goal of the prospective partner: Does the brand need to broaden out a target audience? Examine how the prospective partner's target profile matches yours, using resources such as MRI and SMRB. Due diligence should also undercover any issues with the possible partner that may be a problem (such as they may not be able to pay bills or provide information in a timely manner). The key is to find a matched vision and a partner that wants more than just a transaction—that they want to commit for the "long term" for mutual success. Complimentary corporate cultures will also be helpful to achieve the perfect partnership.
4) **Decide how to build momentum for the association.** Each brand must identify what in particular they can offer partners, and also what strengths they see partner brands contributing. Your brand should have credible reasons supported by research to offer the prospective partner as to how the partnership will be mutually beneficial. For example, a small brand can build credibility by partnering with a bigger, well-known brand. What is in it for the big brand? It might gain some specific skills (the small brand might be a huge presence in the digital sphere) or reach a new target audience from the smaller brand.
5) **Identify resources.** Understand and commit the required resources at the start of the strategic development. Both partners need to have the money, personnel, and leadership

in place in order to devote the time and energy to make the partnership successful.

6) **Negotiate the partnership.** Along with stating the required resources, the brands should commit to their individual responsibilities, in some detail, upfront. For example, you will want to decide whose agency will do the advertising, and which brand will be named first in the communication efforts (or will you alternate?). Everything from how logos are used together to headlines, taglines, press release boilerplates, and particularly social media messaging and engagements should be well-documented and agreed to upon partnership. Brands may jointly create "playbooks" to assist all partners in defining appropriate use and activities within different messages. This is even more important when brand associations are used for lead generation. Lead generation is the initiation of consumer interest or inquiry into products or services of a business, and leads can be used for building contact lists, online communities, or sales. Guidelines need to also focus on the target audience, their behaviors, how analytics will be shared, and how leads will be shared and nurtured.
7) **Be ready to pivot.** Or to say it another way, have an exit strategy. Finally, a successful partnership should bring measurable value to both companies, paying out in terms of direct sales, customer acquisition, marketing efficiencies, and so on. Your partners should be willing to contribute financially or otherwise to the program. While both brands are entering the partnership with good intentions, sometimes things just don't work out—one of the partners gets sold, or decides to go in a different direction. It is necessary to be constantly reviewing the partnership to see if it is effective and if it is indeed a win-win situation—if not, it is time to break off the relationships.

Associating with Causes: Cause Related Marketing

In the early 1980s, American Express introduced a campaign that connected one of their core values directly to a charity: they donated a portion of their profits to restore the Statue of Liberty. Thus was born what is now known as Cause Related Marketing (CRM), an outgrowth of corporate image campaigns where companies and brands present messages about what they value as an institution. American Express' campaign was a success for both the brand and the cause: they increased new cardholders by 45 percent, and card usage increased by 28 percent. More than $1.7 million was donated to restore Lady Liberty.

Cause related marketing is a partnership between a for-profit brand and a nonprofit entity, with the goal of having maximum benefits for each partner. Different types of partnerships include:

- Social issues linked with specific products: The product or service message includes support for a cause, which links the brand with positive associations in the customer's mind. For example, Newman's Own donates profits to a number of different charities including Shining Hope for Communities, Wholesome Waves, and USA Today Make a Difference Day.
- Social issues linked with corporations: Similar to the activities listed above, but the social issue is linked to the parent company rather than a specific brand. Citigroup, a financial services company, promotes its sponsorship with the Human Rights Campaign.
- Corporate donations to specific issues: Advertisers donate a percentage of a product sale to a specific cause. Target donates 1 percent of purchases to schools. MAC Cosmetics donates all of its sales of its Viva Glam lipstick to the MAC AIDS Fund, a separate entity owned by MAC's parent company funding programs that assist with AIDS victims.

CRM has grown as consumers around the globe have become interested in how companies address societal issues. Consumers indicate they buy products associated with good causes, particularly those that address environmental issues and social issues. In addition, several other benefits for brands exist:

- The halo effect: brands will see improved perceptions among audiences who see the cause as a beneficial and important cause

- The brand will be seen as a part of a socially-engaged or responsible company
- The brand will increase its bottom line among people who are interested in supporting the brand AND the cause
- Employee engagement and morale can increase; in addition, team building and leadership can be enhanced by working with the cause
- Brands can receive a tax donation for contributions
- Messages resonate strongly with consumers, and comprehension increases
- Message credibility increases

Benefits for nonprofits participating in associations include:

- Increased funding from brand contributions
- Expanded donor base from brand customers, including new volunteers
- Increased media coverage from brand activities
- Development of earned income opportunities

Some potential downsides of these associations are:

- All customers (and all employees) may not appreciate the nonprofit cause, resulting in decreased attitudes toward the brand
- The brand is likely to have to invest the most resources (time and energy) in such a partnership

The steps in creating these partnerships are similar to the ones for brand partnerships, with a few distinct differences:

1) **Review your own objectives** and be clear on how a CRM partnership will help you meet your objectives. What challenges does your brand face that such a partnership will help you meet? Examine your brand's bandwidth for doing this partnership, because in most cases the responsibility will fall to the for-profit brand to implement this partnership.
2) **Review the institutional fit**—the news is full of CRM partnerships that don't make sense. Examples include nail

polish companies that partner with breast cancer charities—even though many nail polishes contain chemicals that are toxic, hazardous, and contribute to breast cancer. Another example is the fashion company Benetton featuring death row inmates.

3) **Review your key strategic idea** while identifying possible partners. The social issue should be relevant to the company and to the strategic idea. The partnership should also be unique and should not suggest that the company is jumping on the CRM bandwagon because its competitors are doing so.
4) **Conduct due diligence**—the same questions for the brand association work here. There is likely to be a history of partnerships that can be evaluated.
5) **Negotiate the partnership.** What will the cause help with and how much of the work is left up to the brand ? Does the cause need a level of approval over messages?
6) **Create clarity.** The partnership message should be very clear and transparent. Consumers see many of these messages and critically examine messages to evaluate not only the company's commitment to the cause but also to try to figure out what the company will gain from the partnership. Many messages are very vague about the partnership which can easily mislead customers; instead, do your best to demonstrate that the company really does care about the cause.
7) **Provide solutions.** Consumers relate to messages that provide solutions to problems: not only what the company is doing but what consumers can do as well. The brand can discuss how their work with the cause is helping to strengthen the cause's mission.
8) **Track results.** We discuss brand measurement in Chapter 18. Items to track include whether consumers are aware of the partnership, whether they appreciate the message, and how they see the partnership relating to the brand.

Summary

Brand associations can be between two or more for-profit brands for between a brand and a cause (a charity or a nonprofit). These associations should provide benefits for all entities participating in the association and goals should be clarified upfront among all parties. Associations with nonprofit entities provide a unique set of benefits and also a unique set of challenges.

Review Questions

1. What are similarities and differences for a brand associating with another brand and a brand association with a cause?
2. How can "personality fit" between two brands be assessed?
3. What is due diligence? Give an example of something that can be found during due diligence which might cause one brand to not want to partner with another one.
4. What does the term "pivot"' mean? Why is it important for brands to pivot if need be?

Discussion Questions

1. Is the brand association between Tide and Febreze a good association? Why or why not?
2. If Tide was looking for a nonprofit to partner with, what nonprofits might be appropriate? Explain your rationale.
3. If Tide was looking to partner with another brand for a Tide line extension, what brands other than Febreze might be considered? To answer this, think about things that can be added to the wash cycle when you do laundry. Explain your rationale.
4. If M&Ms is looking to partner with another brand to create a new M&M product, what brands could be considered?
5. What kind of reactions do you have personally when you see brands partnering with causes?

Additional Resources

Kotler, P. and N. Lee. 2004. *Corporate Social Responsibility: Doing the Most Good for Your Company and Your Cause*. Hoboken: John Wiley & Sons.

Kunitsky, R. 2011. Partnership Marketing: How to Grow Your Business and Transform Your Brand Through Smart Collaboration. Wiley.

Wikipedia. 2016. Available at https://en.wikipedia.org/wiki/Google_Partners.

Chapter 14

Digital Strategy

Learning Objectives

This chapter is intended to help you:

- Understand what a digital strategy is and what elements it encompasses
- Understand the importance of interactions and two-way communications with customers
- Identify opportunities for data-driven decision making
- Discuss emerging legal and ethical issues

Introduction

Digital strategy is the process of identifying a brand's marketing goals, opportunities, and activities in the digital sphere in order to meet the firm's overall goals for the brand. Today's digital sphere is vast, with new opportunities being created every day. Some brands create a unique strategy for digital; others integrate it into existing marketing. We recommend that the digital strategy be tightly connected to the marketing strategy to create synergy and have all efforts working toward common goals. A digital strategy encompasses:

- Deeper interactions with customers
- Customized and personalized offerings and interactions
- Data-driven decision making
- Organization processes that are reactive to changes in the digital environment

Digital Marketing

Today there are many different ways that we talk marketing in the digital sphere. We previously discussed that many marketing and media plans contain a mix of paid, earned, and owned media. Table 14.1 shows how these different elements operate in the digital sphere.

Table 14.1
Digital Assets by Media Type: Paid, Earned and Owned

Media Type	Definition	Digital Asset	Purpose	Benefits	Challenges
Paid	Brand pays to leverage a channel	Banner ads Paid search Branded content/ native advertising In game ads	Direct people to owned media and create earned media	Immediacy Scale Control	Clutter Declining response rates Poor credibility
Earned	Customers become the channel	Word of mouth	To listen and respond; create ideas for future content and channels	Credible Transparent	No control Can be negative Hard to measure
Owned	Channel a brand controls	Web site Mobile site Social media pages Brand blog Brand Twitter	Create long-term relationships with customers	Control Efficient Versatile	Not as trustworthy as other channels Takes time to scale

Source: http://blogs.forrester.com/interactive_marketing/2009/12/defining-earned-owned-and-paid-media.html.

Because of the vastness of the digital sphere, the digital creative strategy is important, so everyone on the brand team understands where the brand is today and where it wants to go. Clearly, aspects of this strategy will be drawn from the existing marketing plan as we have done throughout this book. Elements of the strategy include:

- The long-term vision, related to marketing objectives
- An inventory of digital assets

- Integration opportunities
- Assessment of core digital competencies
- Creating a vision
- Determining a budget
- Developing an assessment plan

Each of these will be discussed in turn.

The Long-Term Vision

This begins with an assessment of the role of digital in both the development of the brand and contribution to the marketing objectives. Again, the strategy begins by looking at the marketing objectives and matching digital objectives to them. Many brands today focus their digital strategy around a website (owned media). Websites are important since consumers can obtain instant information on products or services to aid them in their crucial purchase decisions. The website, though, should match the strategy of other communications and should blend seamlessly with all other messages customers are hearing. The design of the website should make it clear where people can find the information they need to make decisions.

The long-term vision should also include a content inventory, which is a list of the variety of content that is currently available or will be developed in the next year. This content should be able to be utilized either directly in digital channels or can be repurposed for the digital sphere. For example, many brands do not take advantage of their traditional advertising by leveraging it to other channels online. Many brands put their television commercials on a YouTube channel and call it a day. But these video assets can be utilized in different ways on different channels. These include:

- Utilize television ads on web pages.
- Re-edit ads for a "directors' cut" (a much longer ad) or a shorter clip that could be posted on websites or on social media like Vine and Instagram. This is an example of "native advertising."
- Mobile video consumption is growing rapidly and providing advertisers with a way to reach consumers when they are

paying attention. This trend has been helped along by the expansion of fast 4G/LTE coverage and larger smartphone screens.

With a list of content already available and content to come, it should appear like a "no brainer" to start adding content on a regular basis to a branded website. Some marketers, though, create a static website and rarely update it. Therein lies two problems:

- The first problem is that the days of "if you build it they will come" are over in terms of people finding your website easily. Brand teams should regularly use the Google search engine and perform a search for the brand's name—does the branded website come up at the top (or at least two places from the top)? If it doesn't, and if you are not using any paid media (such as Google Adwords) to promote the site, then it is quite possible that people do not know your website exists. This would suggest that your goals may be to increase both traffic to and time spent on the brand website.
- The second problem is that many brands don't use their branded website to build engagement on the other platforms that consumers use. (A related problem to this is that the brand may not even know what platforms the consumers use—see the section on the "social media audit'" in Chapter 15 for more information on this topic). The branded website should make it clear where else the brand is active in the digital sphere and where consumers can encounter the brand. The website should make it easy for consumers to connect with the brand, such as simple buttons that allow consumers to follow the brand on Twitter or be friends or fans with the brand on Facebook.

Inventory Digital Assets

- The digital asset inventory allows the brand team to identify all the different digital channels used by the brand (a good place to start is seeing what assets listed in Table 14.1 are currently being used). The inventory should include an assessment of the strengths and weaknesses of each channel. Through this analysis, you can determine which digital channels are likely to contribute the most to your goals of sales, engagement, or simply visits to the website; these should be identified.

For most brands, paid media generally perform well against most brand goals. These include:

- Search engine optimization, fuelled by content marketing (organic search results)
- Google AdWords (paid search results)
- Paid ads on social media sites (including promoted posts)
- Email marketing
- Online display advertisements using remarketing: remarketing lets you show ads to people who have visited your website or used your mobile app before. When people leave your website without buying anything, for example, remarketing helps you reconnect with them by showing relevant ads as they browse the web, as they use mobile apps, or as they search on Google.

Every brand is naturally going to be a bit different. This underscores the importance of consumer research to uncover what customers are looking for on your website—and in many cases the customers want answers to their questions quickly in order to make good decisions or to use your product or service appropriately. At the same time, many customers go online because they want to be entertained; many others want to know what is going on in the world (also known as surveillance).

Identify Integration Strengths, Weaknesses, and Opportunities

Research points out that there are five levels of integration, detailed below, going from "least" to "most."

1) Not integrated: digital marketing done on an ad hoc basis.
2) Limited integration: digital marketing is done but it isn't well-integrated into the overall strategy. Inconsistency in one

or more aspects of the messaging between digital and other communications: perhaps the paid media is integrated and the owned media is not.
3) Active attempts at integration: attempts are in place to integrate paid, owned, and earned media with other activities.
4) Fully integrated: digital is seamless from other marketing activities.
5) Optimized: A fully integrated and measuring plan works toward optimization.

A hard look at current efforts should be undertaken and a specific effort toward increasing the integration to one or two levels higher should be clearly stated.

Identify Core Competencies

While some brands relegate much of the digital strategy development to outside agencies, successful brands advocate for sharing responsibilities with in-house teams. Three key areas that brand marketers should always be aware of are:

1) Customer insights, including behaviors, characteristics, and needs. The internal brand team is likely to have immediate access to key digital metrics, and front-line employees (such as customer service reps) are poised to collect information about unfulfilled needs that may help future plans.
2) Strategy: ensuring that paid, owned, and earned digital media are all aligned with a marketing goal. Because many brands using multiple digital assets, it is easy for a brand to create inconsistency in messages.
3) Analysis and optimization: analytics, testing, and post-campaign reviews.

Many brands now use behavioral marketing to a significant extent when developing digital strategy. Behavioral marketing is the use of online data that tracks people's activities to be able to target people who fit your customer persona. It allows brands to profile a specific target (such as people who might switch their cell phone service) based on an analysis of online searches, Internet browsing habits, purchasing history, and much more. This goes beyond the traditional strategy of placing paid messages (such as banner ads) on sites where a brand's target tends to visit. Behavioral data allows brands to target consumers on a range of digital assets.

Related to behavioral targeting is the use of contextual advertising. Contextual advertising examines the website that a user is viewing and then scans the text of a website for keywords that are used to show appropriate ads to the target. So if a potential cell phone switcher is looking at a sports website, the contextual advertising system might look for the keyword "streaming" and if that would appear, an ad for the cell phone provider might appear. Contextual advertising is also used by search engines to display advertisements on their search results pages based on the keywords in the user's query.

Develop a Digital Vision

The key piece of the digital strategy is the creation of a vision on how online assets can fulfill target audiences needs and goals. Most people go online for one of three reasons: to get information, to be entertained, or to be connected. Going back to the original marketing strategy and brand personality, it should be apparent which of these fits in well with your strategy. If you want customers to think of your brand as a friendly brand, you may want to think about providing entertainment options at your site. However, every brand isn't a good fit for entertainment content. The central questions in digital advertising today are: Where will people listen? What content will they engage with?

Prioritizing Initiatives and Developing a Budget

With the wide range of digital assets available, it will be important to prioritize the online initiatives which will achieve the vision. Brands may select one or two initiatives in each category of paid, owned, and earned, but regardless the prioritization involves identifying opportunities that best connect with the brand as well as an assessment of the people needed to make the vision come to light.

Today, many brands have not prioritized mobile, even given that the CMO council reports that 60 percent of all Internet activity in the United States originates from mobile devices and about half of total Internet traffic flows through mobile apps (https://cmocouncil.org/index.php). Also, the website Search Engine Watch reports that 50 percent of all mobile searches are conducted in hopes of finding local results, and 61 percent of those searches result in a purchase (http://searchenginewatch.com/). These two statistics together suggest that any brand that ignores mobile ignores it at its peril and that prioritizing mobile should be an important aspect of a brand's strategy. In fact, a website being optimized for use in the mobile sphere is now a ranking factor for Google's search engine. Any idea that is undertaken for the digital sphere should be undertaken with the idea of mobile in mind. If you wonder whether this is really true, go to any public place and see how many people are looking at their phones. People use their phones to distract them from other things, and when people are already looking at their smartphone, nothing is going to distract them.

Part of prioritization is developing a budget specifically for digital strategy. Having a budget is important because of the need for paid advertising to direct consumers to your digital assets—don't expect it to always happen organically. Additionally, it is not enough to take content developed for traditional media and simply place it in the digital sphere. And this is again where many brands fail—how can these assets be repurposed for use as a digital marketing strategy?

Create Assessment Plans

The final step is to develop an assessment plan. Given that the vast majority of an individual's online activities can be tracked, the list of ways to assess digital plans is long. Choose the assessment tool that best relates to the brand's marketing tool. Table 14.2 identifies several assessment tools based on communication goals.

We will review measurement for other types of social media activities in Chapter 15.

TABLE 14.2
Assesment Tools For Digital Media

Tools	What to Measure	How to Measure
Website	Visits and page views	Measure hourly, daily, weekly Measure where visitors are coming from
	Interactions	Measure number of people who click on content, who respond to surveys, who leave comments in forums
	Sales	Sales per visits
Digital Advertisements such as banner ads	Cost per thousand exposure Cost per click Conversion rate	Compare and track different campaigns
Search Engine optimization	Organic search data Paid search data	Compare different options
Social media: paid ads and promoted messages	Cost per thousand exposure Cost per click Conversion rate	Use analytics available from social media sites

Developing a Digital Team

A digital marketing team will look a bit different from the traditional marketing team as several technical competencies are necessary.

Jason Mogus, Michael Silberman, and Christopher Roy from Stanford University presented four models of digital marketing teams.

1) Informal: with an informal team, digital work is dispersed across various departments and functions. This type of team arose in the early days of digital but today is an inefficient way to work since informal teams lead to brand inconsistency, cost inefficiencies, and a lack of strategy.
2) Centralized: in a centralized team, digital work is placed in a silo separated from other communications activities. The benefits are consistent messaging and branding, common tools, and clear reporting lines. However, a siloed and

centralized team may be slow to respond to change and may not encourage a level of creativity necessary for some brands. Centralized teams also tend to get stuck in a rut of work done well: they can generate a lot of Facebook posts but may not be able to address user experience issues.

3) Independent Teams: with Independent teams, multiple centers of digital leadership are established and different departments are involved in digital activities. Some of this involvement may be seen as somewhat random; some departments may have a digital silo that does well for one part of the business but less well for other parts. Independent teams can create a competitive rather than a collaborative culture, and resources may be duplicated. A single and strong brand message may be lacking.
4) Hybrid: with different business units continuing to build their own capacity based on their specific needs, digital staffers are connected to and supported by a central and strong digital experience team that directs the company toward long-term strategic goals. With this model, the culture of the central digital team is service-oriented and highly collaborative, plus they also have the technical and content expertise to be high-value strategists.

A strong digital team will have people well versed in one or more of these areas:

1) Coding/Programming: the people who know how to implement the vision in the digital sphere
2) Graphic Design: the people who create the visual look of the digital assets
3) Copywriting/Publishing: the people who craft the written content
4) Video Production/Editing: the people who craft the video content
5) Website Management and User Experience: the people who optimize the website so customers have an exceptional experience
6) Mobile Strategy: the people who make sure that the brand's presence on mobile devices matches the brand's other assets

7) Social Media: the people who build connections with customers on social media sites
8) Lead Management/Nurturing: the people who identify the best way to bring people to digital assets
9) Data Analysis: the people who analyze traffic patterns and how people use the site
10) Paid Search Management and SEO: the people who make sure that search engines direct people to the brand's assets

Emerging Legal and Ethical Concerns: Native Advertising

As mentioned earlier, native advertising or branded content is a type of message that matches the form and function of the platform upon which it appears. Native ads are typically long-form blog posts, infographics, or videos that aim to inform, entertain, and inspire people without directly promoting a product. For example, a banner ad from an outdoors retailer might promote parkas, but a native ad from the same retailer might discuss new developments in materials for protective outerwear on the same website where the banner ad appears. Typically, native ads are tagged with a disclaimer such as "sponsored content," "paid post," or "promoted by." The word "native" refers to this coherence of the content with the other media that appears on the platform. Today, younger consumers in particular tend to be put off by ad content that has too much of a hard sell yet are much more open to native advertising. The terms native advertising and branded content are generally interchangeable.

At the end of 2015, the Federal Trade Commission (FTC) published an "enforcement policy statement" on native advertising. Included in the statement was this information:

- "If a natively formatted ad appearing as a news story is inserted into the content stream of a publisher site that customarily offers news and feature articles, reasonable consumers are unlikely to recognize it as an ad.
- Misleading representations or omissions about an advertisement's true nature or source, including that a party other than the sponsoring advertiser is the source of the advertising, are likely to affect consumers' behavior with regard to the advertised product or the advertisement.

- The Commission views as material any misrepresentations that advertising content is a news or feature article, independent product review, investigative report, or scientific research or other information from a scientific or other organization."

What does this means for brands participating in branded content and native advertising initiatives?

- Stronger disclosures from advertisers that are insisted upon by the channel owners. The FTC is likely to hold publishers of misleading native ads responsible, changing a long-standing procedure in the industry. Just having the "sponsored content'" label will no longer be enough. Language like "you may also like this content," which generally points consumers who are reading one piece of content to additional content, tends to be a sponsored placement, and is likely to no longer be allowed by the FTC.
- More differentiation between ads and content—this could very well reduce the effectiveness of such messages in terms of click-through rates and the like. The Internet Advertising Bureau recommends that advertisers and publishers use language that indicates that the advertising has been paid for, even if the message does not contain a traditional advertising message (such as a product sales message). They also recommend that the disclosure be large enough to have people clearly notice it in the context of a given piece of media content, relative to the device it is being viewed on.
- Sponsored posts on Facebook and sponsored tweets on Twitter (and other sponsored opportunities on social media) may no longer be available.

Brands are generally accepting of this new reality, assuming that this new guideline should encourage agencies to up their game on native advertising and provide more creative content. Many think that consumers are focused more on the quality of the content and if the content is good, they don't care where it comes from.

Summary

The digital sphere is rapidly changing and evolving. When developing strategy, though, some basic ideas apply. Digital strategy must relate to overall brand goals and identified brand strengths in the social sphere must be identified. At the same time, brands must keep on top of emerging channels so not to be left out in the cold. Brands must also pay attention to evolving legal and ethical concerns in order to be in compliance with law.

Review Questions

1. What are the strengths and weaknesses of paid, owned, and earned media?
2. What are the five levels of integration?
3. What is native advertising and why did the FTC need to get involved in it?

Discussion Questions

1. Why is it important for brands to integrate messages across digital assets? Are there any downsides to this strategy? When might a brand not want to integrate messages?
2. What are some of the benefits to tracking digital activities? Are there any risks?
3. What brands do you see advertising on mobile? Is mobile advertising different from other types of digital marketing? Why or why not?

Additional Resources

Godin, S. 1999. *Permission Marketing: Turning Customers into Friends*. New York: Simon and Schuster.

Internet Advertising Bureau. n.d. Website. Available at http://www.iab.com/.

Rohrs, J. 2013. *Audience: Marketing in the Age of Subscribers, Fans and Followers*. Hoboken: John Wiley & Sons.

Chapter 15

Social Media Strategy

Learning Objectives

This chapter is intended to help you:

- Understand the unique aspects of social media
- Understand the elements of a social media strategy
- Learn how to do "social listening"
- Assess ways to measure online engagement

Social media is an interesting beast. The term "social media" has become a catch-all term for a variety of different online activities which can be characterized by two distinct aspects—first, both brands and consumers can create content for the site and, second, brands and consumers can interact with each other directly.

Many brands think of social media simply as a message channel and use it tactically to deliver messages. However, because of its ability to develop interactions and the potential to build strong connections between brands and consumers, social media needs a specific strategy. Today, it isn't enough to have a good number of likes or fans or followers—this does not mean that your social media is working. Thinking strategically means connecting social media with a specific objective and undergoing efforts to meet that objective, whether it is generating positive conversations, getting new subscribers, making money, or something else.

Popular Social Media Sites

There are several different types of social media:

- Primarily text-based sites: Twitter, LinkedIn
- Primarily image-based sites: Instagram, Pinterest, Tumblr, Flickr, Snapchat
- Primarily video-based sites: YouTube, Vine
- Multimedia sites: Facebook, Google Plus

A comparison of these different sites is provided in Table 15.1.

Some brands are going to be more clearly suited to image-related sites (such as food, fashion, automotive) and other to a text-related site (such as service providers). But what is more important is where your target audience is going for engagements that you can start and facilitate. As discussed in other chapters, participating in all these social media sites (as well as other digital options as discussed in Chapter 14) is generally impossible for most brands. Building a strong strategy will help brands determine the optimum channels for engagement with consumers.

Developing Social Media Strategy

As with other strategies, there are several steps to developing this strategy:

- Connect social media to an objective
- Conduct a brand audit
- Assess the target audience via social listening
- Translate existing messages into social messages
- Engage and cultivate
- Measure and evaluate

We will discuss each of these in turn.

Connect Social Media with an Objective

The best social media strategies are those that focus (at least initially) on a more narrow rationale for social media. Every brand should have clear goals and objectives that its social media activity is trying to achieve. Often brands select a specific objective relative to engagement that social media will focus on.

Table 15.1
Comparison of Different Types of Social Media

Type of site	Example Platform	Who Is Using It	What Are They Doing on It	Why They Use It	Key Considerations
Multi-media	Facebook	People of all ages, but 65% are aged 35+	Posting photos and text messages Sharing links	To connect with friends and family near and far	Provides easy to use analytics Good for repurposing content, particularly visual content Posting of new content and on page engagement are important to stay "top of feed" People want to stay on site, don't want to leave to look at outside links
Text	Twitter	People of all ages, but primarily 18–29 High usage among urban populations Popular among African-Americans	Tracking current news Following people and brands they like	To engage with content they see as relevant	Powered by hashtags People expect to use links to navigate off-site Currently limited to 140 character messages but that may change Fast paced—constant updates needed
Image	Instagram, Vine, Snapchat	Women aged 35 and younger	Sharing pictures	To upload photos from mobile phones and easily show them to others	Can upload both photos and short videos (3–15 seconds) Easy to integrate with other platforms

Table 15.1 *(continued)*

Video	YouTube	Adults 18–34; reaches more people in that demographic than cable TV	Uploading, watching and sharing videos	Watch original content as well as content from other networks Create and share content	Great way to share information about brands: instructions, testimonials, serial content Include call to action at end of video Plan for responding to negative comments
Story	Blog/Tumblr	¾ of all Internet users read blogs	Education and entertainment about things that interest people	Content is seen as trustworthy, authentic	Integrate into other web materials Ask for comments so people can see that others are engaging with the site

Related to this is the idea that everyone connected with the brand can have an influence on social media. Because of its prevalence, it impacts all aspects of the company. While many brands will have a social media team, involving people from multiple functions in the social media strategy and implementation is important.

Conduct a Social Media Audit

The social media audit is an important tool to understanding where your brand's customers are spending time and what they are doing on those sites. You should investigate what people are saying about your brand on a variety of channels including:

- **A review site like Yelp:** assess what people are saying about your brand and competitive brands. Make notes on both positive and negative information as well as the total number of reviews. This will not only give you information about what challenges your brand faces but also whether you need to develop your presence on the review site relative to other brands.

- **Social media like Facebook:** examine the number of your brand site's followers compared to competitors. Examine the number of posts you make per week and the number of replies to posts, as well as the number of follower posts and shares. Compare these numbers to your competitors.
- **Image sites like YouTube and Instagram:** examine the number of different content pieces you posted during a specific time period compared to your competitors, and the number of responses to each. Also examine the number of people who engage with the content.

Ask yourself how you are doing relative to your competition. What are your strengths relative to competition and where are you lacking? Do you want to increase the presence in weak sites or build engagement in strong sites? Your overall brand goals should guide you to select the optimal strategy.

Assess the Target Audience

Where does your audience spend their time on social media? This simple question can be somewhat challenging because the social media landscape is constantly changing, particularly in terms of how and when people use different social media platforms. Understanding the mix of "established" social media and upcoming social media is important too, especially for brands trying to connect with opinion leaders and trendsetters. There's no point in a brand setting up an official presence on Instagram, Pinterest, or a forum if none of your target audience is there.

Brands should develop social media listening skills in order to figure out what your target is saying about your brand. If a significant amount of people are no longer mentioning your brand, products, or services on a particular platform, ask yourself if your existing strategy and objectives are still relevant for that platform. Social listening is a process similar to a brand audit except it dives deeper into the conversations on your social media sites. Instead of looking at the number of responses to each piece of content you post, examine what you're saying and whether there are any patterns in terms of the things people respond to. For example, do people respond more if you ask a direct question? If you ask people to share content, do they do so? Do they respond more to an image than a text message? Such knowledge can provide insight into building stronger engagements with your social media audience.

In these activities, it is important to include earned and unowned media channels. Never underestimate the power of a brand-related user-generated blog post or a forum full of people who either love or hate the brand. Ignoring unowned and earned media may allow brands to have more control, but it closes the brand off to important opportunities for interactions with potential brand advocates.

Translate Existing Messages into Social Messages

Social media is about engagement and interactions, and as a result the brand personality is arguably more important in social media than in other media. A consumer seeing messages from neighbors, friends, and coworkers will see the brand and to some degree the brand must be seen to encompass personal traits. Many marketing experts preach that passion is the fuel of social media. What this means is that regardless of your position in the market place, your product features and benefits aren't enough to create a passion. How will your organization appeal to the heart of your audience, rather than the head? Think beyond attributes into benefits and values. Disney isn't about movies, it's about magic. Apple isn't about technology, it's about innovation. What are you about?

The value of social media is that you can go beyond traditional messaging and brand image development. You can show how the brand's values connect with customer values, and provide a deeper level of information. You can ask questions related to your message to better understand how your customers interpret it. You can ask your customers to share and help them become opinion leaders. And while your social media strategy has specific goals, remember that your brand is being seen like a person and you don't want to be that person who is constantly bothering someone to buy something. The point of social media is conversation and engagement.

Some brands have used social media as a dumping ground for content created for other channels. Doing so shows a lack of strategy and clear objectives for the respective channel. A press release might be suited for a brand's dot com page, but it may not connect with a Facebook or Tumblr audience. A 140-character post written for Twitter may engage a brand's fans, but that same post should not be posted on other owned channels. For example, depending on the brand's audience, a post on Facebook might be better suited to increase product awareness while one focused on business-to-business networking could be better executed on LinkedIn.

Social media is also more about stories than about brand-focused messages. Several questions to ask when creating content for social media are:

1) What story am I telling?
2) What is the story telling my target customers?
3) Why does my target care about the story?
4) What sort of emotions does the story evoke?
5) How will the story incite action?

Warby Parker's story is about a poor graduate student who lost his glasses on a backpacking trip and couldn't afford to replace them. He spent his first year of grad school squinting his way through class. He (and some friends) realized that there was no easy way to get stylish glass frames at a reasonable cost, and so created a way to do so. The company also allows customers to get several frames delivered to their homes to try on and select. The story is making it easy for customers to be happy with their glasses—and with the company. The company is carbon neutral and partners with nonprofits to get eyewear to people who can't afford glasses. All of the business was created online on their website and promoted through social media—this worked because their audience was online and their story resonated with people.

Engage and Cultivate

A post on social media is only the start of the process. Once you post, hopefully others will respond in a positive way. It is a best practice to respond regularly to consumers' posts—not necessarily to every post, but consumers will want to know that you are listening and being active in the social media sphere. Here are some response rules:

- When someone asks a question, answer them: provide a direct answer to the question or a link to the answer somewhere else. If it is a complex question and answer, arrange to carry on the conversation in a different channel such as email or on the phone.

- When someone complains, apologize and see if the problem can be fixed. If not, apologize again.
- When someone says something nice, thank them.

Measure and Evaluate

Create a Budget: Developing activities and integrating activities is not free: a budget is needed for resourcing which should include training and education of the brand's social media team. Content (whether responsive or broadcast) may also be expensive to produce. Budget is also needed for paid placements on social media sites. Brands that post content and wait for it to "go viral" are likely to be waiting a long time.

Create an Assessment Plan: Finally, as with any strategy, a measurement campaign must be implemented. Social media sites provide tools to help you understand the engagement with your brand (See Table 15. 1 for a list).

It is important to measure:

- Presence: measure of the brand's social footprint
- Influence: branded message adoption
- Perception: emotional reaction to the brand
- Virality: people organically participating in conversations
- Resonance: reaction to the overall conversation about the brand

The ultimate goal of engagement is to create a feedback loop that allows you to meet the goals you set forth in the strategy development phase. All it takes is a little investment of time in order to learn how to properly leverage tools at your disposal. Continual evaluation of your strategy will ensure future effectiveness in your digital marketing efforts. Evaluations also provide information that will allow marketing and PR professionals within your company to better deliver results in future efforts.

Consistency and Flexibility

A social media campaign demands consistency. There needs to be consistency with other message tactics, consistency with the quality and utility of the information, and consistency with your values. There also needs to be a consistency of engagement on social media—customers will not want you to post something and then disappear for days or weeks (or even hours) at a time. You can use a scheduling tool for posts but this removes the brand from the actual interactions.

The timeliness of content must also be considered as part of your strategy. As we have discussed throughout this book, having a mix of long-term and short-term strategies are important for brands, and given that many people turn to social media when news is breaking, figuring out how brands can capitalize on this behavior is important. This phenomenon is known as newsjacking or quickly posting content related to a breaking news story or a trending topic. Oreo is terrific at this type of thing: they tweeted an Oreo-related tweet about the 2013 Super Bowl Power outage. At the same time, newsjacking has worked against brands. A social media campaign to bring awareness to domestic violence used the hashtag #WhyIStayed to share victims' stories. Someone doing the social media for DiGiorno's pizza saw that the hashtag was trending, and apparently without doing further research used the hashtag followed by the words "You had pizza." Twitter users were furious, the tweet was deleted, and DiGiorno sent individual responses to each person who complained about it. To make sure that missteps are avoided, make sure that a rigorous process ensures that newsjacked posts are appropriate for the topic.

This is not the only type of crisis that can occur with social media. As more brands do more on social media, the likelihood of crises occurring increases. Ask yourself if your brand has strategies and processes in place to identify, acknowledge, communicate, and deal with social media crises such as an angry employee post. A brand can plan whatever social campaigns they want, but when they have a crisis on their hands, those campaigns can be worthless if the crisis is not quickly identified and dealt with in a timely manner. The brand's public relations and corporate affairs teams need to be aware of potential social media incidents that could occur and should be involved in any response.

Evaluating New Opportunities

Sometimes it seem like a new social media platform appears every week or so. Some users, especially younger users, get disillusioned once a favored platform becomes too big or corporate; Facebook started to lose some younger users when these people realized that their parents were joining Facebook. How does a brand decide which new opportunities to pursue?

- Costs: new sites should be able to provide CPM estimates for consideration, and these should be at or below the CPMs for existing similar sites (e.g., compare new photo sites to Instagram and new multimedia sites to Facebook). Any variance from the CPM should be clearly rationalized by the new social media site.
- Risk tolerance: new platforms are generally undefined marketing territories, so there is a bit of risk involved in advertising on a new platform. However, being a "first mover" on these platforms could distinguish you from competitors. The downside, though, is that many new platforms fail. Being part of any social media site requires a commitment of resources (time and money) so a plan on how to repurpose content developed for a site that might fail is recommended.
- Resources: many newer sites are designed around constant engagement from users, and that includes brands. In addition to funds, you must be able to invest time and people into developing strategies and maintaining an active presence.
- Demographic fit: most early adopters of new social media are younger users. Brands with younger target audiences are likely to be more successful.
- Product fit: many newer social networks are built around visual content, so brands that are more suited for visual mediums may be more successful.
- Measurement: does the site provide a way to track activities around the brand's involvement in the site? This is a very important way to determine if your investments are worth it.
- Exit strategy: is it fairly simple to get out of your commitment?

Summary

A social media strategy is a compliment to both a brand strategy and a digital strategy. It is designed to reach customers where they spend time in the social sphere and to build engagement with customers. A good social media strategy will enhance relationships and also allow brands to learn a lot about their customers and their responses to message tactics.

Review Questions

1. What is a social media audit? Why is it important?
2. What is social listening? Why is it important?
3. What are five areas important to measure?
4. What is newsjacking? What are its benefits and challenges?

Discussion Questions

1. What are some ways that brands can use traditional media to increase the number of people who like their brand on Facebook?
2. What are some ways that brands can use social media to increase the number of followers a brand has on Twitter?
3. How often do you think brands should engage on social media?
4. What is an important news story happening today, and what is its potential to be newsjacked?

Additional Resources

Heath, C. and D. Heath. 2007. *Made to Stick: Why Some Ideas Survive and Others Survive*. New York: Random House.

Lee, K. 2014. Which Stats Matter: The Definitive Guide to Social Media Metrics. Available at https://blog.bufferapp.com/definitive-guide-social-media-metrics-stats.

Li, C. and B. Solis. 2013. *The Seven Success Factors of Social Business Strategy*. San Francisco: Jossey-Bass.

O'Leary, S., K. Sheehan and S. Lentz. 2011. *Small Business Smarts: Building Brands with Social Media*. Santa Barbara: ABC-Clio.

Chapter 16

Promotional Strategy

Learning Objectives

This chapter is intended to help you:

- Understand the different promotional channels available
- Understand the connection between promotional channels and brand objectives
- Recognize the differences between push and pull strategies
- Understand how different promotional strategies fit into the brand life cycle

Brand messages encompass not only what are considered the primary types of persuasive messages directed to consumers—such as advertising messages and digital messages—but also a range of message delivered through ancillary promotional channels including public relations, sales promotion, direct mail, and sponsorships. When planning strategy for a brand, the amount of time and money needed for these ancillary channels are important to consider upfront. The promotion mix is the mix of all marketing channels used to influence the target market. A mix of both long- and short-term channels are generally used, as well as mix of "push" and "pull" channels.

Push and Pull

Push marketing describes a strategy where businesses take their products to consumers; these strategies include in-store marketing. A great example is a marketing campaign for a new perfume or cologne. Marketers will offer sale incentives to department stores for making sure their new perfume is available to be sampled by consumers. In addition, brands may offer free samples of brand extensions (such as lotion with the same scent) to consumers who purchase the brand. For many customers, this in-store experience is their first experience with the product; many might not even know the product existed before they stepped onto the cosmetic floor. Push marketing is a short-term promotional strategy.

Pull marketing, on the other hand, has the goal of getting customers to come to the brand. Pull marketing includes activities that create brand value and ultimately brand loyalty—to make sure consumers keep coming back to the brand. Thus, pull marketing is a long-term strategy. For our fictional perfume, pull marketing would include traditional advertising that raises awareness of the product especially during gift-giving times like Christmas and Valentine's Day, recognizing that many fragrance purchases are made for gift-giving purposes. This works especially well if the gift giver knows that the gift recipient has already sampled and liked the brand through a push marketing activity such as the one described above. As the fragrance becomes popular and brand extensions are developed, pull marketing can be used to raise awareness of the number of different options available for the fragrance brand.

A brand team might begin with a promotional audit, which is an analysis of the brand's current promotional activities compared to the promotional activities of key competitors. Some categories are promotionally driven: fast food, health, beauty products, and snacks are some top categories. By evaluating both the frequency and type of promotion, it is possible to understand more about customer price sensitivities as well as the types of promotional messages that resonate with them. Some target groups, for example, relate to cents-off coupons—a type of promotion where every customer benefits, albeit for a small amount. Others relate more strongly to contests where a few customers could win tickets to a sporting event—a type of promotion when only a few customers benefit, albeit for a nice prize. There are numerous permutations of these types of promotions, such as the McDonald's Monopoly Game promotion: everyone who buys a product gets a game piece that can lead to a major prize, most people receive a small cents-off incentive.

Promotional Channels

- Traditional Advertising: this term describes long-term strategies to build brand awareness, interest and desire, and includes one-way messages placed in television, radio, newspaper, and outdoor.

- Digital Advertising: this term describes long-term strategies that also build brand awareness, interest, and desire, as well as consumer engagements and interactions; also includes messages placed in the digital sphere on web pages and social media.
- Sales promotion: this term describes short-term incentives to encourage the immediate purchase of a product or service. These can include consumer promotions (incentives given directly to consumers) and trade promotions (incentives given to retailers and wholesalers). Sales promotion activities include coupons (provided via traditional media, online, in-store, or on the product package), in store displays and demonstrations (also known as point-of-purchase activities), sweepstakes, and loyalty programs.
- Public relations: this term describes the art of developing positive relationships with the media in order to generate positive stories about the brand. Media relationships can include traditional channels such as newspapers, magazines, and television talk shows and news programs, and can also include outreach to influential bloggers or other online brand influencers. Tactics include press releases and events. This is a long-term strategy designed to be able to leverage the media when needed, both to talk about positive news about the brand as well as to address any difficulties that the brand is facing.
- Direct marketing: this term describes a short-term strategy of sending a personal message directly to an individual. A number of channels can be used, including letters and catalogues delivered via postal mail and electronic mail. Brands also can contact customers through text messages. Personalizing messages can increase the likelihood that consumers will respond to the message.
- Sponsorship: this is a strategy where the brand pays an organization to feature the brand or logo at an event. In general, brands sponsor events with high profiles in order to be seen by a large audience; we most commonly associate sponsorships with sporting events. As a result, sponsorships can provide

either a short-term strategy (such as sponsorship of a single NASCAR race) or a long-term strategy (such as sponsorship of the National Football League for an entire season).

- Internal communications: many brands will choose to include internal communications in their promotional mix to recognize the importance of this strategic aspect to their business. Internal communication strategies are designed to help organizations achieve their goals by building engagement and understanding among employees.

When considering the promotional mix, difficult decisions may need to be made as all promotional channels cannot be used simultaneously—in general, there are not resources to support such efforts. Therefore, examining where the brand is in its lifecycle can help provide guidance in developing the promotional mix.

The Brand Lifecycle

There are four different stages of a product lifecycle. Different promotional strategies and promotional mixes should be used at each stage to ensure the success and life of the product. Different mixes of long- and short-term strategies should be considered at each stage.

Stage 1—Introduction: when a brand is unknown, the objective will generally be to inform the target audience of its availability in the marketplace. Both push and pull marketing strategies are critical at this stage in order to create awareness and educate consumers about the brand, particularly among segments of the target known as innovators and early adopters. Pull marketing can be used to provide information about the features and benefits of the ad, while couponing and in-store demonstrations can be used as push mechanisms to increase awareness.

Stage 2—Growth: the brand gradually becomes accepted by increasing numbers of people in the target market. Strategic brand efforts help build brand preference as well as to develop customer loyalty. As demand increases, brands may add new distribution channels, meaning that additional sales promotions to the trade may be necessary. Messages are directed to a broader group of consumers.

Stage 3—Maturity: Not all brands make it to the maturity phase, but those that do spend most of their product life at this level. Brands that reach maturity are successful and start to see increased competition; often, some different tactics will be needed to encourage customers to choose this brand over alternative brands. Brands may try to compete with competitors at this point: for example, McDonalds began to offer specialty coffees when the brand saw its breakfast business decrease due to the growth of Starbucks. At this point, push messages will be needed to defend market share and show competitive differences to consumers.

Stage 4—Decline: Not every brand will experience decline; however, some brands do. Decline can occur because the category becomes obsolete (such as VCRs), more innovative products are introduced (smartphones replaced flip phones), or consumer tastes change (most women no longer wear nylons). At this point, marketers have several choices. They can try to revamp the brand by adding new features or uses, market the product only to a loyal niche segment, or discontinue the product. For example, Nabisco repackaged some of its mature products into 100 calorie packs that were appealing to health segments.

Matching Promotions to Objectives

The first step is to evaluate your brand's communication objectives. Certain objectives will work better with certain promotional efforts. Distinguish between long- and short-term objectives and match promotional opportunities that way.

In Chapter 9 we introduced a fictional cell phone provider and showed how their business objectives translated into marketing objectives. We can now add in some promotional strategies that the brand can consider to achieve the objectives, as seen in Table 16.1.

Other brands will have different objectives, of course, and will need to consider different types of promotional strategies. Retail brands with goals to increase customer traffic will need a more specific mix of traditional messages to create awareness and public relations and sales promotion activities (such as coupons and in-store events). Brands that want to encourage repeat business may develop a direct marketing strategy that includes collecting information from customers at the first purchase and then using a sales promotion strategy to incentivize them to make another purchase.

Table 16.1
Integrating Objectives with Promotional Strategy

	Brand Objective	Communication Objective	Promotional Strategy
Brand elements	To increase coverage to 95% of the United States	Create awareness of our coverage strength relative to competitors among 85% of customers over the next six months	This is a relatively long-term strategy that can be accomplished with advertising (both traditional and digital) and public relations
Customers	To provide optimal customer service to all clients	Create knowledge of awards won in customer service area among all consumers over the next year	This may be best served by a public relations strategy using news outlets to announce awards. Additionally, this information could be communicated through a direct marketing strategy
	To increase customer retention by 10% by offering loyalty program	Create desire to continue with the service among 30% of consumers	This is a long-term strategy that is best accomplished with both traditional and digital advertising, and a sales promotion strategy for a new loyalty program
		Increase engagement and interactions on key social media channels with 25% more interactions per week	This may seem like a short-term digital strategy but as the measurement occurs weekly, a consistent social media strategy is necessary
Employees	Increase employee satisfaction with the company by 15%	Create awareness of new channels for interactions so employees know they are heard and supported	This require a short-term internal communications strategy to quickly share information about the channels
		Create awareness of protocols for employee engagement on social media to implement in the next three months	This requires a longer-term internal communications strategy

In Table 16.1, there are two different stakeholders for the campaign: customers and employees. It is possible to develop additional objectives if there are additional stakeholders that should be considered in the marketing plan. For example, a food product might want to consider the grocery trade as a key stakeholder in order to get better shelf or display space. Brands that want to develop word-of-mouth in the digital space might target influential bloggers with special promotions (e.g., a restaurant might offer a free meal to a food blogger). Brands trying to get mentions in the press might consider some special promotions toward journalists.

Consistency and Flexibility

Remember the two watchwords of this book: consistency and flexibility. Maintaining consistency with all the elements of the brand's communication strategy is important: the message should be consistent among all channels that you're using, both in terms of purpose and design. Starting with the objectives and building strategy from them is the optimal way to ensure consistency in communications.

At the same time, flexibility is important to be able to change strategies that are not working and also to take advantage of special opportunities that match that brand values and personality. This means that if objectives aren't being met and as a result strategies need to be reviewed and if necessary, revised. Flexibility also means that the competitive environment must be constantly assessed in order to look for opportunities and protect against competitive threats.

Flexibility also means staying close to customers to listen to their concerns and suggestions. One value of social media, even if the brand is not an active social media user, is that it is possible to gauge consumer reactions to strategies and tactics fairly quickly. Twitter is an excellent source for this—it is possible to search for content that contains your brand name to see what people are talking about. If people don't understand or question your messages, adjustments should be made. Similarly, attending to the employees on the "front lines" of dealing with customers can also provide insight into how the messages are being received.

One way to evaluate this is by determining whether your marketing plan will be considered "fixed" or "flexible." A fixed marketing plan allocates most or your entire budget in advance: committing to specific promotional activities, media placement, and distribution channels for a specified period (for many brands, it's six months or a year). A fixed plan helps you estimate expenses based on projected revenue, and it helps to generate some cost savings by committing upfront to expenditures in media channels. It also ensures a level of consistency among communications.

A flexible marketing plan is based on ideas of what you want to do but gives you the ability to change plans based on the results of the efforts. For example, advertising expenditures can be directly tied into sales results; therefore ad budgets can be established each month. Flexible plans allow brands to respond to marketplace changes and opportunities. It also makes it easier to address problems that arise with the brand. For example, your brand can directly respond to price sensitive customers either by lowering the price of the brand or by changing the message to show consumers why they should pay more for your brand. If response to one promotional channel is strong and others show to be weak then funds can be shifted to the stronger channel. However, too much flexibility can be problematic, as messages are not consistent and consumers may become confused.

Most brands will opt to commit a portion of their budget to being "fixed" while retaining a certain amount to be "flexible" and take advantage of opportunities that arise. These opportunities, of course, must match the overall strategy of the brand.

Common Promotional Strategy Pitfalls

Marketing lore is filled with poor decisions regarding promotional strategies. These include:

- Making assumptions about what customers want. Laura Ashley was a brand that was built around English country lifestyle, and the brand assumed that even as women returned to the workforce in droves they would choose the romantic floral prints for their work wear. They continued this message in traditional channels that quickly lost relevance to working women. This assumption cost them their entire business in the United States and has made them a niche brand in the UK. Rethinking product offerings and selecting a promotional program that addressed women's new working reality might have kept the brand going longer.

- Ignoring the competition: Borders bookstore ignored that other book buying outlets (Amazon and Barnes & Noble, in particular) were introducing eReaders that were tied-in to proprietary content purchases. Borders eventually introduced a poorly performing eReader but failed when they contracted with Amazon to run their online sales operation—ignoring that Amazon would use that opportunity to harvest customers for itself. Basically, Borders used their promotional activities to benefit Amazon instead of the Borders brand.
- Competing on price alone: JC Penney implanted a strategy where instead of using a sales promotion (coupon) strategy, the strategy involved "everyday low prices." Their product offerings were not clearly differentiated from that of other brands with established everyday low price offerings. JC Penney customers had become accustomed to using coupons to shop in the store, and the new price strategy was difficult for customers to adjust to. JC Penney adjusted this strategy shortly after it began.
- Relying on too few customers: the Hummer brand was the largest SUV known to mankind—a positioning that they owned and was clearly unique. However, increased oil prices and the green consumption movement reduced the target to a miniscule size, and the price of the vehicle didn't motivate these customers to replace their Hummers often.
- Trying to grow too quickly: Pets.com was one of the first Internet retailers who allocated a huge budget to promoting their "sock puppet" ad and to building a nationwide warehouse distribution system to service online orders. Unfortunately, the strategy failed to convince consumers that buying pet products online was better than the competition and the company quickly ran out of money. Focusing on a promotional strategy to stimulate first-time and repeat purchases might have saved this company.
- Being complacent and failing to innovate: Firestone Tires lost significant market share when they watched Michelin Tires introduce radial tires to the U.S. market and were slow in creating processes to add radials to their product mix. Promotions started too late to make up for the lack of innovation.

Summary

A variety of promotional channels are available to meet brand objectives. Some channels are suited to particular times in the brand's life cycle, other channels are appropriate for use at any time. Message consistency in all promotional channels is important, as is the flexibility to pivot to other promotional strategies if existing strategies are ineffective.

Review Questions

1. What is the difference between push and pull marketing? Give an example of each.
2. What are the four stages of the brand life cycle and how do these stages influence promotional plans?

Discussion Questions

1. This chapter discussed that a new perfume is likely to use an in-store strategy in its introduction. What types of promotions might be effective as the product moves through its life cycle?
2. Should brands track competitor's promotional strategies? Why or why not?
3. Should promotions for digital-only brands happen only in the digital sphere?

Additional Resources

Diermeier, D. 2011. *Reputation Rules: Strategies for Building Your Company's Most Valuable Asset*. New York: McGraw-Hill.

Gladwell, M. 2000. *The Tipping Point: How Little Things Can Make a Big Difference*. New York: Little, Brown and Company.

Chapter 17

Brand Reputation Strategy

Learning Objectives

- Understand brand reputation
- Understand brand reputation forces
- Understand the online impact on brand reputation
- Understand how to manage a crisis situation

Brand Reputation: Protection vs. Promotion

As you have seen throughout this book, significant effort must be put into developing a strong brand communication program. It requires a cogent brand marketplace position that is brought to life through a strong integrated brand communication plan.

For all the effort put into carefully crafting the plan, it can be undone in a blink of an eye through a myriad of external forces. For example, Volkswagen, the number one auto manufacturer in the world, was found to have deceived environmental regulators in 2015 by deliberately adjusting its emissions software to meet industry standards when they were, in fact, below those standards. One act, such as this, will undo years of building goodwill and consumer trust. This is something that Volkswagon will struggle to get back in the years to come.

Building goodwill and trust among the public is what brand reputation is all about. Brand reputation is based on external stakeholder perceptions. Brand marketing, on the other hand, is based on an internal vision for positioning the brand with its stakeholders. Both reference external audiences, yet they are quite different in their approach.

Brand reputation is about protecting the brand. Brand marketing communication is about promoting the brand. Protection and promotion combine to form the 360 degree view of brand communication. Just like playing basketball or football, you play offense and defense. Brand reputation is building up goodwill so that when a crisis occurs, you have a strong defense. Brand marketing communication builds brand relevancy that leads to increased brand usage. Together, brand reputation and relevancy equal brand equity.

The definition of reputation is "the overall quality of character as seen by others" or "beliefs or opinions generally held for someone or something." A brand's reputation is likely to be two-fold. The first is driven by brand communication. One part of the reputation reflects the brand's marketplace position. Is it associated with being a cheap brand or a quality brand? Is it a popular mainstream brand or is it exclusive? Brand attributes and brand positioning are a key part of the brand's reputation. The stronger the brand's marketplace relevancy, the stronger the brand's reputation.

Digging deeper, the second part of the reputation is the "moral character" of the brand itself. Is this a brand that consumers believe is doing the right thing? Does it act in a fair manner? How ethical is the brand? Brand character forms the basis for protecting the brand's reputation.

A slip up on "moral character" will certainly undo years of work building up the brand's position and relevancy. That is why you need to have a part of your brand communication team measuring, monitoring, and developing plans to enhance your brand's reputation. Equally important is to have plans in place to deal with an external disruption to your brand's reputation.

Forces That Impact Brand Reputation

There are a number of forces that can impact your brand's reputation. You have varying degrees of control over them. The following are three categories of forces that can impact your brand ranked by the degree of control you have over them.

- Direct: Any brand item, communication, or employees
- Indirect: Suppliers and natural materials
- External: Trends, attitudes, third party communication

The first category of forces that can impact your brand include any brand item, your communication, and company or brand employees. In theory, you or someone at the company or working on the brand has direct control of these items. In practice, there are any number of things that can negatively impact your brand that may be out of your control.

As we previously discussed, it is crucial for all communication including personal communication about the brand to be consistent. If the sales force is saying one thing and the advertising is saying something else, then the brand will suffer. With different agency partners and others communicating about the brand, consistency of message is not always an easy task.

Even more damaging than confusion can be when an employee says something derogatory about your brand. While this may not seem like a crisis, in today's digital world, a small comment can be amplified rapidly on social media. Then it takes on a life of its own. Because it is coming from the brand itself, it can have a very strong impact.

Another part of your communication that can be a wild card is if you are using a celebrity endorser. For example, Subway's longtime spokesman, Jared Fogle, was convicted of buying child pornography. Obviously, being a brand associated with child pornography is not what you want. Subway handled the crisis very well. They immediately suspended Jared from their advertising prior to his conviction. Then they divorced themselves of him as the legal process went on.

Indirect forces can also have a major impact on the brand's reputation. Nike suffered a backlash when it was revealed that they were using manufacturing facilities that employed underage workers. Should Nike have done a better job vetting these manufacturing facilities? They certainly should have. On the other hand, it is very difficult to police all the vendors that a brand may be using. This is particularly true of manufacturers who may be sourcing parts of the product from various suppliers all around the world.

From a communication standpoint, you may be using vendors or placing advertising on media properties that may impact your brand's reputation. For example, if you are purchasing digital media using a programmatic buying method, your brand may become aligned with media choices that could either be inappropriate for the brand or bring about negative consumer sentiment. All of a sudden your advertising may appear on an inappropriate website. Or it can be as basic as purchasing broadcast commercials in a television movie of the week, only to then find out at the last minute that the movie contains either graphic sex and violence or a controversial topic such as abortion. Your brand didn't set out to be associated with this type of content. But it can easily happen.

Another area that can have a negative impact on the brand is the sourcing for the raw materials or ingredients. This could be the actual wool to make clothing or mangos to make a sauce. Suppose that growers of mangos are cutting down the Amazon Rainforest. All of a sudden, your brand is a part of a global environment scandal. Or imagine that you are sourcing your wool from a farm that feeds its lambs some biologically-enhanced feed to make softer wool. Now your brand is associated with some form of nonorganic farming.

The lesson is that the brand should develop a checklist for all the vendors in the supply chain. Strategically, the brand should publish their approach to their vendors. Ideally, it would be to the brand's advantage to have a one-page signed agreement with vendors regarding their compliance with your approach. That way the brand has an initial line of defense in case of any incident.

The third big category of forces is items such as societal trends, consumer attitudes, and third-party communication. It can be easy to get sideways with consumer trends and/or attitudes. For example, McDonald's is responding to the environmental movement by making sustainable beef a part of their sourcing for hamburgers. Rather than buck this environmental trend, McDonald's is being a part of it.

Big trends or movements can have a major impact on your brand. This can be environmental trends, dietary trends, or social trends. If you are a cola brand, then you may be on the wrong side of the trend that is moving away from sugary drinks. If your brand is not a part of social media, then you may be left out of the digital conversation. Understanding key trends and putting together a plan to ride the wave is important.

A large threat to your brand is third-party communication. This could be a news article that cites your brand as a prime example of something negative. Or it could be your competition that mentions your brand in its advertising. Monitoring and responding to third-party communication is particularly crucial to maintaining your brand's reputation.

If your brand is attacked either by a third party or the competition, it is vital that the brand act swiftly. If the brand does not respond to an attack, the public will wrongly assume that this third party narrative is true. It is important to nip any third-party brand discussion in the bud. Do not let it linger. The longer it takes to respond, the more vulnerable your brand becomes to further attacks. Plus, that negative view of your brand will linger longer in the public's consciousness.

Online Impact of Brand Reputation

In today's digital world, policing your brand's reputation can be challenging. There are so many channels for consumers, the press, and the public to comment on your brand. It can be overwhelming. That is why you need a team that is constantly monitoring and responding to the online world.

Figure 17.1 shows the major online categories that can impact your brand's reputation. As you review each category, you can see that just monitoring all of these digital categories is quite a task. It requires that you have a search engine optimization (SEO) and social media team working on your behalf.

Figure 17.1
Online Reputation Components

Have you done a search recently for your brand through the top search engines such as Google, Yahoo!, or Bing? What did you find? If you are working for British Petroleum, you might find the following news articles:

- "BP Fraud Case so Massive, Federal Judge Grants Trial Delay"
- " How the BP Oil Rig Blowout Happened"
- "Years of Internal BP Probes Warned of Neglect"

What is mind boggling about this search is that it was done in November 2015. The actual oil rig spill happened more than five years ago on April 20, 2010. Yet, if you just searched for BP, it was like the oil spill happened yesterday. Clearly, BP needs a team to better optimize their search results.

The key to optimizing search is to continue to develop content that raises your brand to the top of the search topic. Strategically, new content coupled with a small pay-per-click campaign can drive results that the brand would want to attach to its name. Otherwise, like BP, you are leaving it to chance.

Optimizing your brand's search results is an ongoing process. It is particularly crucial when the brand has encountered some negative press or event. Take action to ensure that your brand is seen in the best possible light. That means aggressively developing content that counteracts negative stories about the brand. Have a strong voice in how your brand is perceived in the marketplace.

Your social media team should be actively monitoring the competition, social media platforms, blog sites, forums, and review sites. All of these media platforms offer the opportunity for anyone to post negative comments about the brand.

The first line of defense in social media is to be on the offense. That means being active on social media sites that are important to your customers. This may mean publishing white papers on forum sites or contracting with an influencer to write a blog that includes the brand. Whatever the communication, make sure to identify that it is coming from the brand. You should be as transparent as possible on social media. If you are not, the pain of being found out as a brand that is "trying to dupe" the public can be swift and severe. A little common sense goes a long way when developing a social media strategy. Content is king.

The more active the brand becomes, the greater the defense of negative comments.

Review sites exist for nearly every product category or for every company. Some review the brand or product and other sites provide reviews of what it is like to work at the company. All of these review sites can impact your brand's reputation. So, what happens if someone writes a negative review? The best strategy is to address it head-on. Acknowledge the reviewer with humility. Then provide an action plan to correct the negative review.

Consumers are getting savvy to the fact that reviews may not be from "real customers." Sometimes a competitor may write a negative review or on the other hand, a friend of the brand may write a positive review. There are now review sites that review the review sites. It is a bit maddening. Regardless of the one-up man ship on review sites, keep to the tact of acknowledgement and action. Consumers view that in a positive way. It takes the edge off of negative reviews.

Whether it is digital, print, or broadcast, the press can have a big impact on your brand. The deeper you go on the Internet, the less credentialed the journalism. News sites, like any media business, build their business based on the size of their audience. A bigger audience translates to more advertising revenue. To get a bigger audience sometimes means that these news sites may sensationalize the news. That is where you need public relations counsel. When a news site begins to attack your brand, it is crucial for the public relations team to act. This is to ensure that the brand's side of any story is heard. And it means to ensure that the facts are presented without speculation. This requires diligence upon the public relations team to make sure that no negative news story goes unchallenged. Just as we saw in the BP search example, if you let news items linger, it will have a long-lasting negative impact on your brand.

Managing a Crisis Situation

If you do not have a plan for a crisis situation, that alone is a crisis. Every brand needs to be prepared for a crisis. If you are managing the communication for an airline, you need to know to be prepared if there is a crash. If you are managing communication for a restaurant chain, you need to be prepared if a customer gets food poisoning. Or if you are managing an auto brand, you need to be ready for items such as if the car's braking system requires an immediate recall. These are just a few of many examples of a brand in a crisis situation.

A crisis is something that must be dealt with quickly and professionally. This is not a situation that you want to leave to chance. Strategically, the first step before you have to respond to a crisis is to develop a plan and a team that will implement the plan.

A crisis management team should be established for the brand well ahead of a crisis. This is crucial since a crisis situation requires initial rapid response. So, everyone must know their role and be ready to react as a unit.

Most crisis communication teams consist of the brand communication manager, legal counsel, financial management, human resources, and possibly a risk management director (if the company or brand has one). Depending upon the company, the CEO, COO, or President may elect to be part of the team. Obviously, senior management must be kept in the loop in any crisis situation.

The plan should consist of three key elements:

1) Immediately reduce the tension of the crisis.
2) Commit the company or brand to a course of action.
3) Control the flow and accuracy of communication.

The key to dealing with any crisis situation is to acknowledge it and attempt to reduce the tension that it has created. For example, when Volkswagen was found to have used software in its vehicles to skirt the emissions laws, it waited three days to respond. And when it responded, it did not acknowledge that the problem was widespread. It was initially thought to be only on diesel vehicles. Then it was discovered to be on other vehicles and all VW brands, such as Audi.

The lack of transparency in their slow response added even more damage to an already damaging situation. What should VW have done? The first step would be to immediately acknowledge the problem. Step two would have been to say that they were committed to a rapid and deep investigation for all makes and models of VW. VW needed to act in good faith. The third step would be to report on what they found. Control the bad news or someone else will control it for you.

In any crisis situation, you must do what is right. That may mean that there is a serious financial consequence to your actions. For example, in the BP Gulf of Mexico oil spill, BP spent literally billions of dollars in restitution. If BP had been quicker to respond to their crisis, this situation may not have been nearly this costly.

There are also potential legal consequences to a crisis. That is why it is crucial to have legal counsel present to review any communication. Communication, if poorly managed, can come back to you as a lawsuit. This is particularly true if the company or brand is negligent in any way.

Keep a small team of rapid responders ready to manage the brand through the crisis. It is much more effective to have a single point person for external communication than to rely on a group effort. Take action. Be transparent. Follow through on the company or brand's commitment. By doing these three items, the brand should be able to weather the storm and come back stronger than ever.

Summary

In summary, managing your brand's reputation is a key part of the 360 degree brand communication process. Brand reputation protects the character of your brand. It provides a compliment to the promotion of the brand through marketing communication.

To effectively manage the brand's reputation, it is important to monitor outside forces that can potentially impact the brand. These include direct, indirect, and external forces. Some of these forces are long-term trends while other forces are suppliers or your own communication. In any case, it is crucial to have a plan and take action if you see that an outside force could have a negative impact on your brand's reputation.

The online world presents a complicating factor for brand reputation. There are a myriad of online forums, bloggers, journalists, review sites, social media, and general online chatter that can impact the brand. Like any outside force, it is important to acknowledge and act toward any negative influence. With online communication, it is crucial to maintain brand integrity and transparency.

Always have a plan for a crisis situation. To be prepared in the event of a crisis, form a crisis team. This team should consist of a senior communication manager, legal counsel, human resources representative, and a finance person. When a crisis happens, the first step is to immediately reduce the tension of the situation. The second step is to put forth a plan of action. Third is to control the flow of communication.

Brand marketing campaigns come and go. A brand's reputation is long-lasting. It is in the best interest of the brand to be careful to guard its reputation. It is one of the key components to long-term brand success.

Review Questions

1. What is the definition of brand reputation?
2. How does reputation management differ from brand marketing and positioning?
3. What are the three major forces that can impact your brand's reputation? How much control do you have over these forces?
4. What is the impact of online media channels regarding a brand's reputation?
5. What are the key categories that impact the brand from an online perspective?
6. What is crisis communication? What steps should you take to deal with a crisis?

Discussion Questions

1. What makes the brand's reputation different from the brand's position in the marketplace?
2. Give some examples of brands that have a clear market position yet have a poor reputation. What do they have in common?
3. Go to a review site such as Yelp. Find a brand that has poor reviews. What are they doing to combat these reviews? What might you do differently?
4. Find a digital news site such as the Drudge Report that has strong opinions about various topics. Do you find that these news sites only tell one side of a story? Give an example.
5. What is an example of a brand facing a crisis? How did they handle it? What could they have done better?

Additional Resources

Moriarty, S., N. Mitchell, W. Wells. 2014. *Advertising & IMC: Principles and* Practice. 10th ed. New York: Prentice Hall, New York.

Fink, S. 2013. *Crisis Management: The Definitive Guide to Managing the Message*. New York: McGraw-Hill.

Lukaszewski, J. 1992. *Influencing Public Attitudes: Strategies That Reduce the Media's* Power. Brookfield, CT: Rothstein Press.

Lukaszewski, J. 2013. *Lukaszewski on Crisis Communication: What Your CEO Needs to Know About Reputation Risk and Crisis Management*. Brookfield, CT: Rothstein Press.

Chapter 18

Measuring Success

Learning Objectives

This chapter is intended to help you:

- Understand components of brand communication measurement
- Understand message and creative measurement
- Understand awareness, attitude, and usage measurement
- Understand brand reputation measurement
- Understand marketing measures and modeling
- Understand media measures and impact

Components of Brand Communication Measurement

If you can't measure it, you can't manage it. Peter Drucker, a famous management thinker used that saying quite often. Mr. Drucker has published an extensive body of work regarding productivity and efficiency. The first step in his process was to determine how best to measure the process. Otherwise, how would you know if you are successful?

This is especially true in brand communication. If you don't know what success looks like, someone else may define it for you. Brand communication has many stakeholders and many people quick to offer an opinion. Without a well-crafted measurement strategic plan, you are like a ship without a rudder. It goes with the wind. In this case, it may be a windy senior manager or board member.

Figure 18.1 details the components of brand communication measurement. We've identified five broad areas for strategic measure. Each of these areas answers a broad question about your brand communication program.

Figure 18.1 Components of Brand Communication Measurement
1. Messaging Message Framing/Positioning Reatice Expression **2. Market Impact** Awareness Attitude Usage **3. Reputation** Perception **4. Marketing Measures** Traffic or Buy Rate Sales **5. Media Impact** Delivery Efficiency Social Website

- Message: Is your message compelling and executed in an equally compelling manner?
- Market Impact: What is the market impact of your brand communication program?
- Reputation: What is the brand reputation impact of your program?
- Marketing Measures: What is the business impact of your program?
- Media Impact: What is the media impact of your program?

All of these areas are crucial to the success of your brand communication program. You can't have a win in one area and a loss in another and consider your communication program a success. They must all work together to build brand equity.

For example, you may craft a compelling message and over-the-top creative expression of that message that generates high market impact yet doesn't move the needle in terms of business metrics and erodes the brand's reputation. The 2015 KFC campaign that brought back Colonel Sanders is a classic example of this. It generated a lot of buzz yet for the wrong reason, alienating its core family customer base and negatively impacting its brand reputation. KFC quickly changed course with its portrayal of Colonel Sanders to help reverse the situation.

Developing a research plan to measure each of these areas is the first step. Strategically, you want to develop a system that helps identify areas of opportunity that you can impact before they become a problem. To effectively do this, it is important to understand the relationship between these measures.

There are communication measures such as messaging and media. There are brand measures such as market impact and reputation. And there are marketing or business measures such as buy rate and sales.

Figure 18.2 provides a visual representation of how each of these areas impacts the other. Communication provides the fuel for brand success. Communication measures therefore can help predict the marketplace success of the brand. The weaker the communication program, the weaker the marketplace impact. Brand measures are predictors of business success. The stronger the brand measures, the stronger the business results.

In the book, *Brand Immortality* by Hamish Pringle and Peter Field, the authors provide a checklist of brand metrics that correlate to business success at each stage of a brand's product life cycle. In their description of these correlations, the authors identify brand measures as leading indicators of success and business metrics as lagging indicators of success.

The concept of leading and lagging indicators is an important one for a brand communication professional. That is because much of brand communication is focused on ultimately achieving business metrics. If brand sales are down, many times that is a symptom of a brand or communication problem. So, the quicker you understand the communication and brand dynamics of the brand, the quicker you can head off a problem that will impact the business.

Figure 18.2
Measurement Predicators of Success

Communication

↓

Brand

↓

Business

Let's review each of these five areas with an eye on how to develop a strategically sound method for measuring and predicting success.

Message and Creative Measurement

It is easy to get caught up in the creative execution of brand and miss the central point of brand communication. That point is that the message you deliver must be distinct, compelling, and motivate the target market to take the appropriate action. No matter how interesting or intrusive the creative execution, if the message isn't right, then you will have a less than successful effort.

The message goes back to how the brand is positioned and how its value proposition is framed to the target market. Strategically, you want to ensure that the most compelling aspect of the brand is promoted. The way to do this is through value proposition testing. In its simplest form, value proposition testing can be done by having consumers react to various statements about the brand. Here is an example for Crisco cooking oil:

- Crisco is the number one brand of cooking oil used by millions of women and loved by their families.
- Crisco is the original brand of cooking oil trusted for over 100 years by generations of women.
- Crisco is always the same consistency which means that your dishes come out right every time.

In the above case, you can get a read if positioning Crisco as the most popular, having the greatest heritage, or being the most consistent product is the best approach. This type of testing is a precursor to creative development.

A simple worded value proposition test may be effective for a consumer package good product such as Crisco cooking oil. It may fall a bit flat for a brand where you are trying to convey a very deep sense of emotion. It is hard to image that Nike did simple value proposition testing to land of the idea of "original athletic performance."

Another way to test broader ideas or more emotional value propositions is through a similar exercise using video. For example, you can ask your advertising firm to create a short video that captures authenticity or grit and determination and then compare that to a video of a product/feature demonstration. By using video, you can amplify the emotional tenor of the position. This helps to gauge the consumer's reaction to the message.

Once you have your message, value proposition, or big idea, you are ready to turn your attention to the best way to express it. You will want to evaluate some alternatives on how best to express your idea. At this stage of the process, it is important to challenge the advertising agency or your creative group to shoot for some unexpected ways to express the idea. This is the time to experiment and try new ways of communicating. Rather than making "creative testing" an exam, treat it as a laboratory for innovation. Many advertising agency creative heads abhor creative testing since they believe that it stifles creativity rather than promotes it. It is important to ensure that you have a method that provides you the information required to make a strong decision and a format that the creative team will buy into.

Copytesting is the term that covers a broad range of advertising creative testing. There are a number of research companies that provide copytesting services. All have their own methods for evaluating advertising.

One of the jobs of brand communication is to have a clear viewpoint on what you expect the advertising to do and how advertising works.

For example, is your message designed to change an attitude about the brand? Or is it designed to switch a competitive user? Both are valid objectives. Each one is very different and may require a different method for determining the best approach.

We are learning much more now than ever before on how advertising and any type of persuasive communication works. A new wave of research that employs technology that measures the psychophysiology of the brain can aid in better understanding the emotional connection of a brand message and the consumer.

Companies such as Sensory Logic that use a combination of galvanic skin response, facial coding, and a written diagnostic can provide deep understanding of the emotional connection to any advertising stimuli. Others such as NeuroFocus use MRI technology to understand the brain activity level of various stimuli and also provide learning about the emotional connection to your campaign.

With such an array of methods and tools to better understand the reaction of messages and creative execution, it is incumbent upon the brand communication director to use these resources to maximize the message and creative connection to the target market.

Awareness Attitude and Usage

Most brands have some form of an ongoing tracking study to understand the communication impact of their campaign. These studies typically measure awareness, attitude, and usage (AAU) of the brand. Sometimes they are called AAU studies or Brand Health Tracking Studies. All seek to understand the ongoing impact of the brand communication campaign in the marketplace. For the sake of discussion, we will call these AAU studies.

The AAU study provides strong learning on how a campaign impacts the top of the brand purchase funnel. Figure 18.3 shows a typical brand purchase funnel and the methods used to measure each part of the funnel.

Awareness is the top of the funnel. The AAU tracking study provides a solid measure of total awareness of the brand but more importantly, it is the first mention or top of mind awareness. Unaided awareness or top-of-mind awareness is a leading indicator of brand success. An example of a

Figure 18.3
AAU Measure with Brand Purchase Funnel

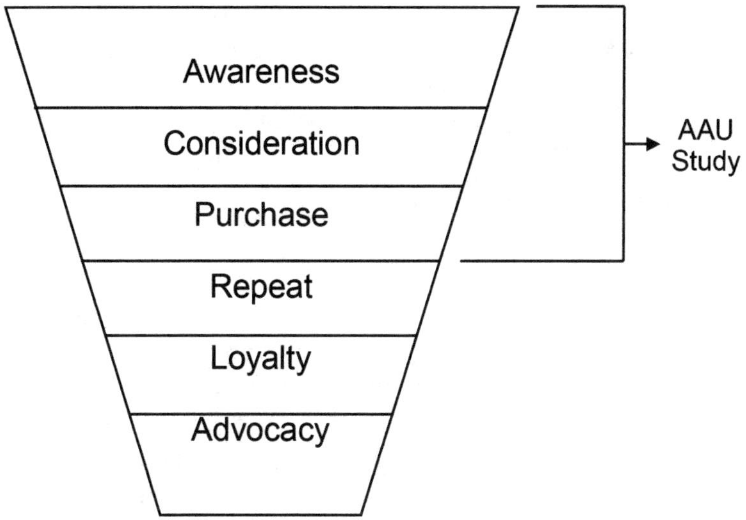

top-of-mind question is: "When you think of trucks, what brand comes to mind?" Perhaps your answer is Dodge or Chevy or Ford. Regardless, the first brand mentioned is highly correlated to the market share leader. If you can drive first mention for an unaided awareness question, that has tremendous marketplace value.

The second aspect of the AAU tracking study is attitude. This is the attitude that the consumer may hold for your brand. Within the attitude section of the study are diagnostics that you hope to improve. For example, you may ask consumers if your brand is perceived as high quality or fairly priced or sexy. The tracking response to either product attribute or brand personality provides clues on how the brand may perform in the marketplace.

The third aspect of the AAU tracking study is usage. Usage provides a variety of diagnostics. The first stage of usage is consideration. Is your brand in the considered set when a consumer is thinking about making a purchase in the category? For example, if the Dodge truck is not in the considered set when a consumer is thinking of purchasing a truck, that provides learning on what part of the purchase funnel to direct your attention. The second stage of usage is how likely the consumer will be to purchase the brand. This is also called purchase intent. The third stage of usage is purchase.

Ideally, these types of studies will be fielded on a weekly or at minimum monthly basis. By constantly monitoring these aspects of the brand communication campaign, you can not only measure success but understand how to adjust your plan to meet the changing nature of the consumer. Timely measurement will provide you with the insights needed to act and react to marketplace conditions.

Brand Reputation

There can be confusion in tracking a brand's reputation versus the consumer's attitudes toward purchasing the brand. There is certainly overlap. Yet there are some key distinctions. For example, measuring how the brand performs in the category on product attributes such as price, quality, and performance factor into a brand's reputation. A brand's personality also contributes to a brand's reputation. These factors can and should be measured in the ongoing brand tracking study or AAU study. They help provide input into the reputation of the brand.

Reputation measures are deeper and sometimes more complex than the standard ongoing tracking of a brand's purchase intention. For example, let's take the case of Walmart. Walmart is known for being a low price leader. In an ongoing tracking study, you may measure price as a variable. Does being the low price leader mean providing comparable goods at a lower price than the competition or does it mean providing less quality goods than the competition? Do people think that Walmart will stop at nothing to be the low price leader such as source their goods from a country that does not have child labor laws?

Is Walmart's reputation for low price built on an ethical model or on an unethical model? That is the deeper part of a brand's reputation. Brand reputation impacts a wider set of stakeholders than a brand purchase tracking study. It includes suppliers, shareholders, and employees of the company. The focus of a brand's reputation is aligned with brand values and doing the right thing.

This means that the brand should develop a reputation management study that tracks deeper issues that can have a longer-term impact on the brand. This may mean adjusting the study to account for changing values. For example, understanding the sourcing of goods has become more important to today's consumer. This may be an area to understand how the brand is perceived in the market. Brand reputation studies work hand-in-glove with ongoing AAU studies to provide a full view of how the brand is viewed in the marketplace.

Marketing Measures and Modeling

Like it or not, sales will become a measure for brand communication. So, it is important to understand the components of sales for your brand or organization. The basic components for all brands are the same. Sales is a function of the number of buyers multiplied by the amount that they buy. There are nuances by industry. More importantly, every brand has slightly different objectives on how to grow sales or revenue. It is crucial for the brand communicator to understand the role that brand communication may play in generating sales.

In the retail industry, sales are calculated by the traffic (number of consumers coming to the store or website) multiplied by the average ticket (average amount spent per transaction). A retail brand can focus on its outward communication to drive traffic and work either in-store or online to add more to each transaction. Just think about how Amazon offers up more ideas for you to purchase once you make a buy on their website. That is an example of trying to increase the average transaction. On the other hand, when a department store such as Macy's promotes a one-day sale, this is an example of driving consumers to the store or to increase traffic.

Typically, brand communication focuses on bringing consumers to the store regardless if it is brick-and-mortar or online. If you have a role in the website or social media transactional platforms, then you may work both sides of the sales equation.

In the consumer package goods industry, sales are calculated by penetration (the number of people buying the brand) and buy rate (the average number of times the consumer purchases the brand). Like retail, most brand communication is directed to get more people to try the brand. However, for certain products, there may be an emphasis on buy rate or usage of the brand. Trial is the objective when a brand introduces something new to its product line such as a new flavor. Then the role of brand communication is clear. It is to gain adoption of that new product. Gaining increased usage is important to brands or products that have a high penetration yet an infrequent usage. For example, WD-40 (the spray lubricant) is found in most garages or home utility cabinets. The trick for WD-40 is to get people to use it in a variety of ways. Otherwise, it just sits on the shelf until a need arises. Brand communication in this case is to promote more needs.

Business-to-business sales (B2B) can be different than that of either retail or consumer goods. Retail and consumer goods are very transactional. The consumer shops, buys something, and then uses it. In B2B marketing, the buyer may enter into a long-term agreement or contract with the seller. Depending upon the business, the buyer may be looking for more of a relationship than just a simple transaction. As a result, while buying a tube of toothpaste is a frequent purchase, a business-to-business transaction may take months or even years to complete. And the transaction may be consummated by a salesperson or even senior management. While sales may be computed the same as retail and consumer goods, the sale can be very different. So, the role that brand communication may play in such an industry can be different as well.

The other aspect of business metrics is margin or profit margin. This is the amount of profit made on each item sold. Maintaining or increasing a brand's profit margin is the goal of any brand. It shows that the brand has strong value in the marketplace. If your brand operates at a higher profit margin than competing brands in your category, this tells the financial community that your brand may be worth a premium as security equity. Margin is a key indicator of the health of the brand. So, protecting a brand's profit margin can become an important role for brand communication.

Understanding how the brand's business metrics can be influenced by communication is vital to measuring the success of the brand communication. To help answer this question, brands are turning to sophisticated statistical methods to develop a model that will isolate the impact that brand communication has on brand sales.

The ability to develop powerful models that can isolate the effect of variables on sales is increasingly available due to the continued flow of information. Consumer transactional data is available now on a daily and sometimes minute-by-minute basis. By harnessing this data and combining it with the brand tracking information, social media, and website metrics, you can develop an econometric model that can not only isolate communication effects but help predict future impact.

Your mission is to ensure that tools such as econometric modeling are used properly. One shortcoming of such models is that the information is all based on the past. While understanding the past is valuable, it is not an infallible predictor of the future.

Paid, Earned, and Owned Media Measures

One other broad area of measurement for brand communication lies with the use of media. As we have previously mentioned, there are three categories of media: paid, earned, and owned. Each should have its own metrics to evaluate the tactical implementation of the brand communication plan.

The fundamental measures for a paid media campaign are delivery and cost efficiency. You should have metrics for the delivery of the campaign that fall into three camps:

1) Impressions: The total number of exposures for the campaign. This is a great benchmark for a variety of comparisons including last year's plan, alternative plans, and the ultimate delivery of this year's plan.
2) Reach and Frequency: The percent of your target market that is potentially exposed to the campaign with the average number of times exposed. This puts some dimension to the total impressions.
3) Effective Exposure: The percent of your target that is effectively reached with the schedule. You may want to determine with your media team the appropriate frequency level or range that is deemed to be effective.

Cost efficiency can be done by calculating a cost per thousand analyses on the plan using the impressions from the plan delivery. The formula for CPM is Cost/delivery × 1000. This analysis tells you how much you are investing to reach 1,000 people or 1,000 of your target market. This is also a good benchmark to compare plan purchase to delivery or to compare historical plans to this year's plan. Both delivery and cost efficiency are excellent metrics that measure the tactical effectiveness of your paid media effort.

Earned media are those impressions generated by a third party. These can be the result of a public relations program and/or as a result of other media activity. Media coverage through public relations can be measured by the number of outlets that carried the story and their respective total audiences. Brand mentions on social media or other media platforms can be evaluated by research companies that track and organize this activity.

Owned media consists of media that you control such as your website and/or social media. Or it could be other media or even events. From a digital perspective, you should measure the reach of your owned media. This can be done by tracking the number of followers of your social media platforms and the number of visits to your website.

For social media platforms, you should also measure engagement through the number of likes, retweets, and/or participation. You should periodically track the social media sentiment for your brand. A sentiment analysis determines the positive versus negative comments made about your brand on social media. This is an important piece of information.

For the website, you should measure the bounce rate and time spent on the site. The bounce rate is the percentage of people who click on your website and then leave after just viewing your home page. A high bounce rate tells you that you may need to develop more compelling content. A time spent analysis will provide deeper diagnostics on which pages people find the most compelling. All owned media is a work in progress. You should be constantly monitoring and adjusting your owned media to more deeply engage your target market.

Media measurement provides the tools to adjust the tactical elements of your brand communication program. Like other measures, media measures should be viewed not as just a report card but rather insights into how you can continually improve your brand communication program.

Summary

In summary, measurement impacts every facet of a brand communication program from conception to market impact. Strategically, measurement should be viewed as a path to insights and not just a scorecard. It is important to develop measures that can be actionable. For message and creative development, that means to conduct separate research measures for message development and creative execution. The same holds true when developing research methods to measure market impact and reputation of the brand communication program. The market impact measures should align with the brand purchase funnel while reputation measures should align with brand values. All marketing activity including brand communication will ultimately be judged largely on the contribution to overall sales and profitability. It is important to understand the role that brand communication plays in the business. From this understanding, a cogent research plan can be developed that isolates the communication contribution to business success. Measuring paid, earned, and owned media provides ongoing tactical learning to be used to constantly adjust and better the brand communication program.

Review Questions

1. What are the five components of brand communication measurement?
2. What is the difference between message and creative testing?
3. How are awareness, attitude, and usage interrelated?
4. What is the difference between attitude and reputation?
5. What is marketing mix modeling? How is it used?
6. What are key metrics for social media and website?

Discussion Questions

1. The authors have identified five broad categories of brand communication measurement. Can you think of any other areas that should be considered?
2. Should brand communication always be tied to business metrics? Can you think of examples of this?
3. When is digital engagement more of a predictor of success than traditional AAU measures?

Additional Resources

Hill, D. 2007. *Emotionomics: Leveraging Emotions for Business Success*. Philadelphia: Adams.

Kelley, L. and D. Jugenheimer. 2015. *Advertising Account Planning:*

Planning and Managing an IMC Campaign. 3rd ed. New York: Routledge.

Pringle, H. and P. Field. 2009. *Brand Immortality: How Brands Can Live Long and Prosper.* London: Institute of Practitioners in Advertising.

Surowiecki, J. 2005. *The Wisdom of Crowds*. New York. Anchor.

Tellis, G. 2003. *Effective Advertising: Understanding When, How and Why Advertising Works,* Newbury Park, CA: Sage.

Index

Italic page references indicate photographs, figures, and tables.

About the Authors

Larry Kelley is a Professor of Advertising at the Jack J. Valenti School of Communication and has been in the advertising industry as a practitioner for over twenty-five years. Professor Kelley most recently was Executive Vice President, Chief Planning Officer of FKM and has served in senior management roles for BBDO, Bozell & Jacobs and the Bloom Agency. He is the author or co-author of eight books adopted in hundreds of college and university programs, including programs in Brazil and Korea.

Kim Bartel Sheehan is a Professor at the University of Oregon where she also directs the Honors Program in the School of Journalism and Communication. She has over twelve years of agency experience on accounts including McDonald's and Kraft. She is the author or co-author of eleven books and dozens of academic articles in journals such as *First Monday, Journal of Advertising, Journal of Public Policy and Marketing,* and *The Information Society.*